❧ GETTING STARTED IN ❧
BIRDWATCHING

Edward W. Cronin, Jr.

❧ GETTING STARTED IN ❧
BIRDWATCHING

Illustrated by
Gordon Morrison

HOUGHTON MIFFLIN COMPANY ◆ BOSTON

*To my parents
and to Siggy, who gave me
the idea in the first place.*

For information about permission to reproduce
selections from this book, write to Permissions,
Houghton Mifflin Company, 215 Park Avenue South,
New York, New York 10003.

Library of Congress Cataloging-in-Publication Data

Cronin, Edward W.
Getting started in birdwatching.
1. Bird watching. 2. Bird watching—United States.
I. Title.
QL677.5.C78   1986   598'.07'234   85-30572
ISBN 0-395-97637-5

Printed in the United States of America

QUM 10 9 8 7 6 5 4 3 2 1

CONTENTS

❧ GETTING STARTED IN ❧
BIRDWATCHING

❧ INTRODUCTION ❧

How does a beginner start to identify birds? Typically, the birds he sees are moving so fast through the foliage or across the sky that he seldom gets a good view. When a bird does pause for a second, the beginner often is frustrated in attempting to compare what he sees before him to the drawings in the field guide. His guide might have several hundred illustrations of different birds, species descriptions, family descriptions, notes on habitat, ranges, maps, etc. He starts flipping frantically through his book, looking at the bird, looking at pages—looking at the bird, looking at the pages. His bird disappears, a new one comes into view, the page flipping begins again. He saw something like that in his book before but now he can't find it. He can't focus his binoculars. The bird keeps moving. The pages keep flipping, The bird keeps moving. He thinks he has it. One more look. The bird disappears. Ahhhhh. . . . .

By contrast, the knowledgeable birdwatcher walks two steps into the field and identifies a dozen species in as many seconds, calling them out as fast as he can pronounce their names. The beginner stands in awe, dumbfounded.

Our beginner comes to wonder whether he lacks some special talent or is hindered by inferior eyesight and hearing. He feels overwhelmed by the field guide; he feels uncertain about his ability. Many people become so disappointed and defeated that they give up completely and thereby miss out on a lifetime of enjoyment.

How does the experienced birdwatcher do it? It is true that he is familiar enough with the common species of his neighborhood that he can identify them with the same rapidity that we can recognize a friendly voice on the phone, or a relative walking some distance away. An experienced birder's detailed knowledge has been acquired by years of study, hard work, and constant birding.

But the fact of the matter is that a competent birder can go anywhere in the world and, armed with a good field guide, identify 80 percent of the birds he sees without hesitation. Even in a foreign land where the birds are new, he demonstrates remarkable proficiency. The key to his success is that he knows *how*. He has taken the time to acquire some basic skills and has matched them with a fundamental understanding of the methods of field identification. His magician's trick of rapidly identifying species is, in truth, based on a logical procedure that anyone can master.

This book is dedicated to explaining the "how" of bird identification. It is not a field guide (if you don't have one already, you will need to buy one; see page 59 for some hints) nor a book about birds, their appearance, or behavior. Rather, it focuses on the techniques of birding, the tricks of the trade which are so obvious to experienced birders that they are often forgotten and seldom mentioned.

This is the beginner's beginning book, and it outlines a systematic approach that will enable you to identify birds in your backyard or throughout the country. I have tried to keep the book concise. There is much that can be said, but I want to concentrate only on what you'll need to get started and avoid repeating material covered in other books.

Most field guides, for example, explain about range maps, notations used to describe vocalizations, terminology used to describe the parts of a bird, and so forth. Look to your field guide for this information. Also, you might need to consult a dictionary for the definition of some terms, such as the biological meaning of *family* or *species.* And there are many general books that list places to go birding, describe how to use bird feeders, and offer more expansive discussions on the life history and behavior of birds.

By contrast, this book has a very narrow scope. I will judge it a success if it does help some beginners overcome the frustration of using a field guide for the first time. Birding is just too much fun to be missed because of bad technique or a poor introduction.

To my mind, birding is a delicious combination of outdoor exercise and intellectual activity. Once the basic techniques are mastered, it becomes addictive with its varied pleasures: the fresh air and scenery; the great adventure game of identifying species; exploring new country and new lands; views of the most beautiful creatures on the face of the earth; and the constantly expanding awareness of the natural world. It's really worth doing — when you know *how*.

PART I

THE THEORY

❧ THE THEORY ❧

After several years of teaching beginners, I have learned that their biggest problem is that they make things too difficult for themselves. They are their own worst enemies. They'll either jump in the middle of a field guide, expecting to figure it out as they go along, or they'll choose an identification problem — say, migrating fall warblers — that would give a professional ornithologist a headache.

Learning to identify birds is like learning how to use a phone book. In fact, phone books and field guides have a lot in common. Each is a long list of items arranged in a logical order, although the order is very different. I don't know anyone who tries to look up a phone number by beginning on page one, column one, and reading each entry — name by name by name. I do know of a lot of people who try to use a field guide this way.

In essence, there is a right and a wrong way to identify birds. A little time spent learning the right way before you start out to do it, can make all the difference. Perhaps the single most important thing I have to say, the essence of this whole book, is that you should start birding with your head, not outside with your feet, chasing fall warblers.

A little time spent learning the right way to identify birds can make all the difference. Start birding indoors with your head, not outdoors with your feet.

To this end, the first step is to learn what I will call the **Theory of Elimination.** This is the core of the identification technique and its most important feature is that it involves a calculated process of examining the possibilities rather than a random process of trial and error.

THE THEORY OF ELIMINATION

Eliminate as many species as possible from consideration before you attempt to identify anything.

In other words, first determine what the bird *can't* be before you consider what it *can* be.

There are about 700 species of birds in North America, and to consider each one when making an identification takes too much time, effort, and energy. Yet this is exactly what many people do as they search through their field guide, comparing each illustration with their unknown bird. Instead, you should consciously narrow down the possibilities.

How? There are a series of simple tests that can help you determine whether a bird should, or should not, be considered. Much of this work can be done at home with your field guide before you even begin to watch birds. Additional tests can be applied as you are observing the bird, in an efficient, step-by-step method that takes advantage of brief observations.

All of these tests can be thought of as the *tools* of the identification process. The *process* itself is one of elimination. You want to be constantly reducing the number of birds you must consider to as few as possible, so that your final task of species identification is relatively easy. At the moment of truth, as your unknown bird offers a final brief view, you want to be choosing between a few or perhaps half a dozen possibilities at most, not six hundred.

There are three basic tests. Let me outline them first to give you a general idea, and I will explain them in detail later. I have listed them in a descending order of importance, but as you gain skill and familiarity with the birds you will be able to apply the tests almost simultaneously, if not immediately.

Test 1: Location

Eliminate all birds not found in your **geographic area, elevation, season,** or **habitat.**

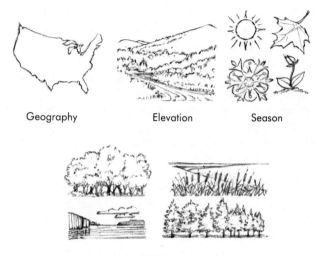

Geography   Elevation   Season

Habitat

Test 1: Apply the location test first. Narrow down your choices by ruling out all birds not found in your area at this time of year.

Test 2: Characters of the Family

Eliminate certain families of birds from consideration by ruling out those whose members lack the same general appearance (**body shape, size, bill, legs, behavior,** etc.) as the bird you are trying to identify.

Test 3: Characters of the Species

Finally, choose between the remaining possibilities based on **specific details,** such as the color of the breast or the presence of wing bars.

Shape   Size   Bills

Feet   Behavior

Test 2: *Try to figure out which family your mystery bird belongs to. The type of bill or legs and feet can be an important clue. Notice how the bird behaves as well as its overall size and shape.*

ROSE-
BREASTED
GROSBEAK

RUFOUS-SIDED TOWHEE

Test 3: *Turn to your field guide to compare the field marks that distinguish the remaining birds under consideration. Does your bird have eye-rings or an eye-stripe? Is there a pattern on its wings or breast?*

Before you lift your binoculars to examine an unknown bird, you already know a lot about it. Indeed, you know perhaps the single most useful character for its identification: *you know where it lives.*

Never underestimate the value of this information. It is critical to rapid field identification.

This is because birds are not evenly distributed across the continent. They may vary according to geography; some birds are confined to the northern states, some are found only in the South; some only in the East, and some only in the West. A few are found only in a single state, and many are spread across the entire continent.

They vary with the seasons; many species visit North America only during the summer, and some are strictly winter visitors to the U.S. Some birds are resident throughout the year in a particular area, while others might use different areas each season.

They vary by habitat; there are birds found only in deserts and others are found only in dense forests. Some require a very specific habitat, yet others can be found in almost any habitat.

And finally, they vary according to altitude; there are birds which favor the lowlands and others which are found regularly on mountain tops.

Thus, although there are some 700 species of birds scattered throughout North America during the four seasons, it is highly unlikely that you would ever see more than a hundred at any one time in any one place. Let's look at some examples.

1. Geography (Range):

There are fifteen species of hummingbird found in America, but a person observing a hummingbird in New England can immediately suspect that it is a Ruby-throated Hummingbird, as this is the only species regularly found in the Northeast.

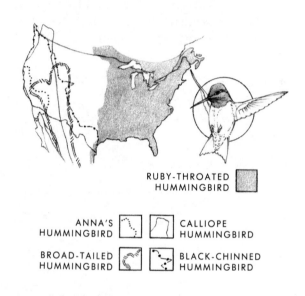

RUBY-THROATED
HUMMINGBIRD

ANNA'S
HUMMINGBIRD

CALLIOPE
HUMMINGBIRD

BROAD-TAILED
HUMMINGBIRD

BLACK-CHINNED
HUMMINGBIRD

The location test simplifies your choices: Although there are a number of hummingbirds west of the Mississippi, the Ruby-throated Hummingbird is the only species regularly found in the Northeast.

2. Elevation:

The height above sea level can also be a good clue for a particular species. A thrush seen on a mountain top (i.e., above 2500 feet) in New England would likely be a Swainson's or Gray-cheeked Thrush, as both these species favor higher elevations there. Conversely, it is unlikely that either of these species would commonly be found along a valley of the Connecticut River, where the Wood Thrush, Veery, and Robin predominate.

SWAINSON'S THRUSH

WOOD THRUSH

If you know you've seen or heard a thrush, but you're not sure which species it is, check the habitat preferences of different thrushes.

3. Season:

Many birds have distinctive seasonal movements and migrate each year between a northern breeding ground and a southern wintering area. In my own state of Vermont, for instance, we rarely see Tree

Sparrows during the summer months. They are common in winter, early in the spring, and in late fall, but during the summer they are usually found only in their far northern breeding grounds in Canada.

SPRING–TREE SPARROW

SUMMER –
COMMON YELLOWTHROAT

FALL–RUFFED GROUSE

WINTER–DARK-EYED JUNCO

Seasonal variations. The regional checklists at the back of this book will help you learn which birds are year-round residents or breeding birds in your area, and which ones visit it only during migration or in winter. The same type of habitat can provide food, cover, or nesting sites for different birds at different times of year.

4. Habitat:

Many birds live only in specific habitats, such as fields, hedgerows, forests, seashore, and alder swamps. In summer the Bobolink, for instance, is primarily a bird of the open fields and pastures,

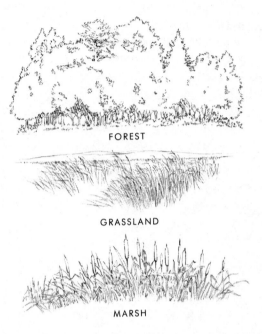

FOREST

GRASSLAND

MARSH

*Woodlands, grasslands, and marshes all support differ-
ent types of birds. Learn which birds are associated with
the different types of habitat in your area. Although
some changes can be expected during migration, if you
know which birds generally are not found in a certain
type of habitat, you can concentrate on the ones that are
likely to be found there.*

while the Ovenbird is generally found only in deciduous woods or dense thickets. In fact, entire families of birds are often confined to a limited habitat
type. Rails are birds of the marshes and estuaries;
you would not expect to find one in sagebrush
desert.

There is much useful information available on
the distribution of birds, but how do you take ad-

vantage of it efficiently? When you are in the field straining to identify birds quickly, there is just not enough time to analyze it all. Even range maps can take too much time to use. The task, then, is to organize your book in a convenient way before you go birding.

Spend a little time at home with your field guide and a red pen or a yellow highlighter. Go through the book species by species and place a conspicuous mark beside those birds which are regularly found in your birding area, perhaps your county or state.

What you want to do is personalize your book, making it the ultimate local field guide. Your notes can make your book significantly more useful and efficient.

Similar marks can be made designating season or habitat. Invent your own system of notation. I use a letter code, and place it next to the picture of each bird, where I can see it immediately: "W" for winter visitors, "R" for year-round residents, "B" for summer residents that breed in the area, etc. I use a double set of letters for habitat: "SS" for seashore, "SB" for scrub brush, "DS" for desert, etc.

The code "B–DW" beside the American Redstart in my book, for example, tells me at a glance that the bird is a summer resident of my area and it favors deciduous woods. If a bird doesn't have a code beside its picture, I know I probably don't need to consider it while birding in my area.

Besides your field guide, checklists are a good source of information on bird distribution. These are comprehensive listings of the birds of a particular area and are extremely convenient, especially if they are annotated. I have included nine checklists in Part III of this volume. There is one for each of the major regions of the continental U.S., and they are cross-referenced according to habitat. An introduction (p. 65) explains how to use the checklists.

Your local birding society is probably the best source of data on the birds of your specific area. They often have individual state or county checklists, and can provide details about local elevation trends. Put all of these notes right in your field guide where they belong and can be used efficiently.

Your personalized book is now a greatly improved field guide. You are, perhaps for the first time, really ready to go birding. It's time to let you in on

The First
Great Secret of Birdwatching:

It is what it appears to be!

The natural tendency of most beginners is to question each identification. This is a healthy attitude in general, but often beginners will question themselves right out of the correct identification. At different times, I have seen a humble pigeon standing in front of a class of beginners transformed into a Lesser Prairie Chicken, an immature Inca Dove, and even a Spruce Grouse. Doubt creates possibilities, and the imagination runs wild.

The first great secret of birdwatching: the bird is what it appears to be—in this case, a pigeon, not a grouse.

Yes, you are playing the odds if you identify a certain species, such as the Ruby-throated Hummingbird, based on geography and habitat and perhaps a quick view. You might have missed something. Sure, it might be a Lucifer Hummingbird, normally found only in the Chisos Mountains of Texas but now suddenly wandering the suburbs of Grand Rapids, Michigan. It might even be the first record of a new and unknown species recently evolved because of toxic waste. But the point is — it probably isn't.

For now, for the first few weeks of birding, take advantage of the odds and don't go looking for trouble. Your field guide is based on the work of thousands of competent birders who devoted their lives to producing an accurate and comprehensive book. Recognize that rarities are just that: rare. The bird before you is probably a common species and is, quite honestly, exactly what it appears to be.

Finally, let's do a quick analysis to demonstrate how powerful the Theory of Elimination is when used with just the first test — **location.** Say you're about to go birding in a Vermont marsh during the summer. Before you take one soggy step into the field, you can use the techniques mentioned above to prepare yourself.

If you got out your field guide and started counting — putting a mark beside only those species found in Vermont, during the summer, at a marsh, and eliminating all others — the numbers would go something like this:

⤳ SUMMER MARSH BIRDS OF VERMONT ⤲		
Total North American birds	about	702
Minus non-Vermont birds	−	380
Vermont birds	about	322
Minus winter birds	−	145
Vermont summer residents (breeding birds)	about	177
Minus birds not found in marshes	−	130
Vermont marsh birds (summer)	about	47

As you walk bravely toward the marsh, binoculars in hand, there are really only 47 species that you need consider. Knowing this gives you more than just confidence, it gives you the "right stuff." You have a manageable list you can use to begin to identify birds intelligently. It's time for congratulations. You've just learned 50 percent of the art of rapid field identification.

⤳ TEST 2: CHARACTERS OF THE FAMILY ⤲

Having a manageable list is a significant aid, but in the previous example, there are still 47 possibilities to consider — 47 birds that you must decide between. Some birds will be easy to identify: the Common Crow, the Belted Kingfisher. But what about those small brownish things flitting through the cattails?

BELTED KINGFISHER

COMMON CROW

Unfortunately, you are now face-to-face with the ultimate dilemma in bird identification — you must begin to learn your birds! Don't despair. There is an easy way: *learn the family characters first.*

There is no need to memorize the plumage of every species in the book. Your next priority should be to learn the basic characters of each bird *family* so that you can quickly place an unknown bird into the right family. The family test, like the location test, can help you eliminate species, reduce the number of possibilities, and make the final task of identification relatively easy.

Even after we've applied the location test, that small brown bird in the cattails might be any one of 20 or 30 possible species. But if we can identify its family, we might well be able to narrow it down to one of only two or three species. The final identification would then be relatively simple and significantly faster.

CROW

OWL

DUCK

HAWK

Learning the bird families is not all that difficult. If you already know the difference between a crow, an owl, a hawk, and a duck, you already know how to recognize four families. Your task will be to learn a little, not a lot, about 50 or so of the common American bird families. You don't need to become the world's expert on vireos. All you need to do is be able to spot a vireo when you see one.

Most field guides include a brief introduction to each bird family describing the basic attributes of that family; a few hours spent studying these sections will be sufficient. Roger Tory Peterson gives a particularly good description of each North American bird family in his Field Guides.

Note, however, that many families are divided further into subfamilies or even smaller groups. The icterid family, for example, can be readily broken up

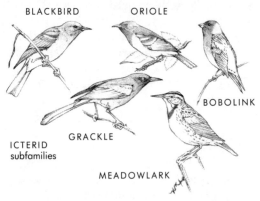

BLACKBIRD   ORIOLE

BOBOLINK

ICTERID
subfamilies   GRACKLE

MEADOWLARK

into several distinct subgroups: the blackbirds, the grackles, the orioles, and two unusual species, the Bobolink and the Meadowlark. The smaller the grouping you can place your unknown bird into, the easier it will be to make an identification.

When using family information, recognize that it is usually a combination of very few characters that identifies a family. Often it will be a general outline, such as a particular bill shape, body profile, or posture. Behavior is sometimes important.

Among the numerous songbirds, the greatest difficulties are often with the three large groups comprising the flycatchers, warblers, and sparrows. It is a tremendous help to be able to place a bird, if appropriate, into one of these families. Only a few characters are needed to separate one family from another and in learning them you should concentrate on the distinguishing points described below:

1. Flycatchers:

Small birds with upright postures that typically sit on exposed perches, from which they fly out on short sorties to capture insects in midair. Flycatchers are relatively passive in their behavior compared to warblers; they are generally olive or gray in coloration, without the striking colors often common in warblers.

2. Warblers:

Small birds that generally have a horizontal posture when perched and typically move quickly and constantly within the foliage. Many are quite colorful as adults. All the species have small, slender bills, well adapted to picking insects off the leaves and branches. (Vireos, another family of small songbirds, are similar to warblers in size and posture but are usually less active. The shape of the bill is also slightly different: in vireos, the bill has a curved ridge that ends in a slight hook.)

3. Sparrows:

Small birds, sometimes brightly colored, but more commonly grayish brown with streaking. Their most notable feature is a short conical bill, which is diagnostic for the group and which is useful for cracking open seeds, a principal part of their diet.

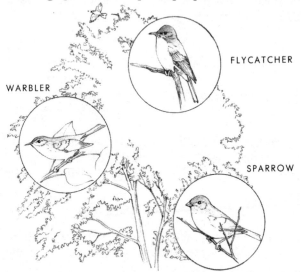

FLYCATCHER

WARBLER

SPARROW

Small birds are usually the most difficult to identify. Learn to tell whether a bird is a sparrow, a warbler, or a flycatcher, and you will be well on your way to an identification. If your bird doesn't belong to one of these three families, that will help you eliminate many species from consideration.

If these descriptions leave you feeling somewhat uneasy, you're not alone nor the first to feel that way. On one hand the differences between these families are very obvious to any experienced birder; but on the other hand, they are based on subtleties of shape and behavior. They become meaningful only in the context of what constitutes a small bird, or a slender bill, or an upright posture. There's nothing like knowing your birds in order to identify birds.

Before you give up, fearful that there's just too much to learn for a part-time birder like yourself, let me explain

The Second
Great Secret of Birdwatching:

---

*What you don't see is as important
as what you do see.*

If you listen carefully to experienced birders, you'll hear them saying things like, "Well, it was too big to be a warbler, so I looked at the fall plumages of . . ."

Or, "The bill wasn't right for a thrush. It had to be a . . ."

In essence, they back themselves into an identification. They know enough to know when some-

*The second great secret of birdwatching: what you don't see is as important as what you do see. If the bird's bill is the wrong size or shape, for example, you know what it **isn't**, even if you haven't figured out yet what it **is**.*

thing is not right. When a character is missing. Or when a significant feature is absent. They know that the absence of a character is as important as the presence of a character.

The only way of acquiring this ability is to treat the birds as a whole and try to learn something about at least one bird in *every* family. If you have limited time available for study, proportion your efforts throughout the book rather than devoting all your time to a single family. In practice, by learning a little bit about each family, you will end up knowing a lot about every family (see tips on p. 46).

- ◆ If you know a Robin or a Bluebird, you know a thrush.

- ◆ If you know a Goldfinch or a Cardinal, you can learn the other finches — and what makes a finch different from a warbler.

- ◆ If you know one warbler, you can learn the others — and how to tell the warblers from other small songbirds.

- ◆ If you know a Kingbird, you know a fly-catcher (see p. 33).

Start with the most common and familiar birds, then branch out to the more challenging ones. Try to learn something about each family, but concentrate on those birds that are most likely to be found in your area.

↘ TEST 3 : CHARACTERS OF THE SPECIES ↙

You know your families. It's time to take the last step — the final identification **of the individual species.** You're standing in Vermont, during the summer, in a marsh; this location information enables you to narrow the possibilities down to less than 50 birds. You see a small, brown bird with a slender, slightly downcurved bill and a cocked tail;

that combination of characters points to a member of the wren family. You look carefully at the bird. It has to be a . . .

Stop! There are two classic errors at this stage which each of us has to repeat until we learn better. I'm embarrassed to admit that I'm still a repeater.

First, we tend to concentrate on the appearance of the bird while completely ignoring its behavior and voice, which are equally, if not more, serviceable clues for identification.

Second, we try to see everything and take mental notes on every aspect of its plumage — the color of its head, chin, neck, back, breast, wings, etc. If we've reached this stage in the identification process correctly, there is no need for a feather-by-feather analysis of our bird. Instead, we should be looking for a few specific traits or field marks which vary from family to family.

The simplest way to avoid both faults is to understand that watching birds involves more than just pointing your binoculars at a bird. The whole time your eyes and ears are taking in information, your brain is analyzing it and weeding out some details so you can concentrate on the rest.

If your interest is aesthetic enjoyment, then by all means relax and view the bird casually for its own sake. But if your goal is identification, then you should make viewing the bird a deliberate process, a calculated mental effort. You can identify birds much more efficiently if you take advantage of

The Third and Final
Great Secret of Birdwatching:

Before you look, know what you're looking for.

Lift your binoculars with a purpose. Discipline yourself to think about why you are looking, what you expect to see, and what you hope to gain from it. Exercise your intellectual abilities, not just your idle curiosities.

The third great secret: *Check your field guide first, so you will know which field marks to focus on with your binoculars.*

If you're about to choose between two or three possible species, you should know how you are going to choose *before* you look. You should be alert to the variety of clues a bird can provide — diverse features that include not only appearance, but also behavior and vocalizations.

Take the present case for example, the wrens. There are two Vermont marsh wrens. One species, the Marsh Wren, has a bright white eyebrow and white streaking on its back. The other, the Sedge Wren, has a buffy eyebrow and nondescript streaking on its back.

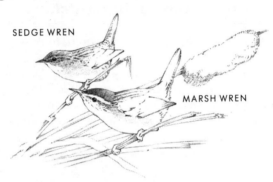

SEDGE WREN

MARSH WREN

If you knew that these markings are the only characters needed for making a species identification, think of how much time you could save. One quick view, for a few seconds, would be enough to identify the species. Does it have a white or buffy eyebrow? What does its back look like?

As a beginner, you will have to check your field guide each time to determine the important characters. The best field guides, such as Roger Tory Peterson's, make this task relatively easy. The text accompanying each species emphasizes these characters, while the illustrations use arrows that point directly to the diagnostic features. With such aids, you can analyze the identification problem quickly and know exactly what to look for.

The extra minute spent looking at your book is worth ten minutes spent idly looking at the bird. Even if the bird disappears before you can identify it, your effort will not have been in vain. You will have learned what to check for the next time you encounter this particular problem.

And you'll be learning in the most productive way. Instead of rote memorization, you'll be learning bird-by-bird within a logical framework, so that each experience builds upon the last to form an expanding knowledge of the birds. You'll be learning the birds not as isolated species divorced from each other, but as a whole within which each species is known by the way it resembles or differs from the others.

It will take you a while to match skills with experienced birders across the nation, but you'll be surprised how fast you can become the resident pro of your local area.

Let's take a moment to examine each of the three categories of clues for species identification — appearance, behavior, and vocalizations.

1. *Appearance:*

Once you have placed the bird in the correct family, focus your attention next on the *differences* between species rather than on the overall appearance of any one species. (As you become more experienced, you will find that these differences add up — quickly and subconsciously — to a distinctive overall impression that identifies the bird.)

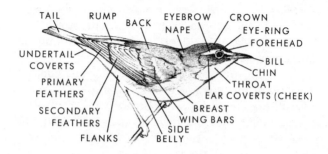

It is helpful to learn the names for the different parts of a bird's body.

Usually, a combination of two or three characters will separate species within a family or subgroup. To tell the vireos apart, for example, you must note the coloration of the chin and breast; whether the bird has eye-rings, whiskers, or eyestripes; and the appearance of its forehead and crown.

The warblers can be separated into two groups—those with wing bars, and those without. The sparrows can be divided into those with breast streaks and those without.

Sometimes, a single character will cut through an entire family, effectively separating the family into two subgroups. The warblers, for example, can be divided depending on the presence or absence of wing bars; the sparrows can be broken down into two groups based on the presence or absence of streaking on the breast.

More rarely, a single character will prove sufficient for the identification of an individual species within a family. The only flycatcher with a white band on the tip of its tail is the Eastern Kingbird. The only chickadee with a white eyebrow is the Mountain Chickadee.

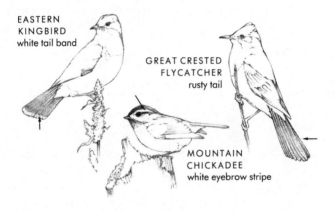

EASTERN
KINGBIRD
white tail band

GREAT CRESTED
FLYCATCHER
rusty tail

MOUNTAIN
CHICKADEE
white eyebrow stripe

Keep in mind that you usually don't have to choose between all species of a family — many will have already been eliminated by the location test. Also, you can evolve shorthand rules for certain birds in your area. For example, the only flycatcher in New England with a rusty tail is the Great Crested Flycatcher.

2. Behavior:

Behavioral clues can be very useful in identifying birds. The movement of a bird is much more easily seen than a particular color or pattern of its plumage. The better field guides include notes on behavior, especially specific and characteristic patterns of flight, feeding movements, or posture.

Certain flycatchers, for example, can be identified by their tendency to wag their tails. Certain warblers can be identified by their habit of feeding primarily on the trunks of trees or, conversely, on the ground. Flickers and Goldfinches can be told by their undulating flight patterns, while Meadowlarks fly in short glides between rapid wingbeats.

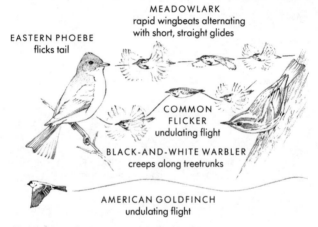

MEADOWLARK
rapid wingbeats alternating
with short, straight glides

EASTERN PHOEBE
flicks tail

COMMON
FLICKER
undulating flight

BLACK-AND-WHITE WARBLER
creeps along treetrunks

AMERICAN GOLDFINCH
undulating flight

Distinctive behavior and flight patterns can help you identify birds, usually without lifting your binoculars.

3. Vocalizations:

The calls and songs of birds can be extremely helpful; indeed, many experienced birders rely on sound clues for a majority of their identifications. Sound carries well and is not susceptible to the vagaries of changing light conditions or the obstacles of vegetation. Whether the bird is perched in the open or concealed in the trees or brush, its song or call note can tip you off as to what bird to look for. Records and cassettes can help you learn the calls and songs of different species.

There are even some species that can be effectively identified in the field only through their vocalizations. The Empidonax flycatchers, for instance, can be told apart somewhat on the basis of their habitat preferences, but otherwise they look so much alike that positive identification depends on their distinctive songs. Many of the thrushes live in the forest, where dense vegetation makes them difficult to see; their songs, however, are easy to hear and to tell apart, once you have learned them (see p. 56).

⤳ THE THEORY AT WORK

In discussing each of the separate components of the identification process, we may have lost the sense of the process itself. As a review, let's follow a specific example from beginning to end, to see how the theory of elimination — as applied to the location (step 1), the characters of the family (step 2), and the characters of the species (steps 3–5) — can guide us to a final identification. Let's go birding on a warm summer morning in Vermont.

1. Location:

Half our work should be done before we even enter the field. Our field guide lists over 450 species, but we can eliminate some 275 based on geography and season. Our personalized field guide has been clearly marked so that we need only consider those birds that are summer residents of Vermont. That leaves us with **about 175 birds to consider.**

2. *Appearance and behavior (family characters):*

We observe a medium-sized, black-and-white bird clinging to the side of a tree. On our first quick view we note that the general profile is that of a woodpecker: the bird has a straight, pointed bill and is clinging to the tree with its feet and propping itself up with its stiff, pointed tail feathers. The bird's behavior of digging into the bark with its bill is also typical of woodpeckers. The only other families that could be considered (i.e., birds that cling to the side of trees) are the nuthatches and the creepers, but the nuthatches' tails are too short and are never used as a prop, and the only creeper found in North America is too small and has a decurved (down-curved) bill.

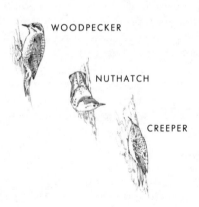

WOODPECKER

NUTHATCH

CREEPER

Checking the woodpecker family in our anno-tated field guide, we note that there are **8 wood-peckers to consider.**

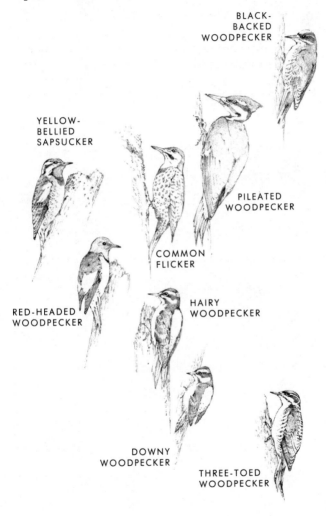

BLACK-
BACKED
WOODPECKER

YELLOW-
BELLIED
SAPSUCKER

PILEATED
WOODPECKER

COMMON
FLICKER

RED-HEADED
WOODPECKER

HAIRY
WOODPECKER

DOWNY
WOODPECKER

THREE-TOED
WOODPECKER

3. Appearance and behavior (species characters):

From our original quick view, we remember that the bird was a medium-sized, black-and-white species. As we scan the woodpecker illustrations, we see that two species don't fit at all — we can eliminate the Flicker, which is too brown, and the Pileated Woodpecker, which is too big. Now we have **only 6 woodpeckers to consider.**

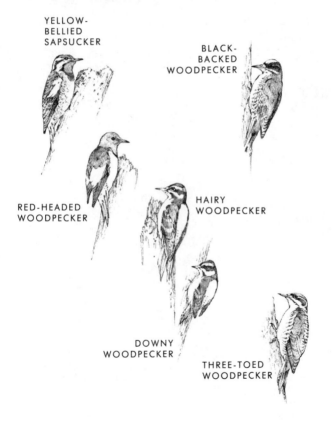

YELLOW-BELLIED SAPSUCKER

BLACK-BACKED WOODPECKER

RED-HEADED WOODPECKER

HAIRY WOODPECKER

DOWNY WOODPECKER

THREE-TOED WOODPECKER

4. *Field marks:*

It's time to take a second look at the bird, but first we should find out what to look for. In our field guide, we can see that the remaining species can be most easily distinguished by the coloration of the back and wings. On our second quick view, we see that our bird has a barred, black-and-white back without any wing stripe. We can now eliminate the Yellow-bellied Sapsucker and the Red-headed Woodpecker, which both have large white wing patches. It can't be a Downy nor a Hairy, because they both have a uniform white back. And it can't be a Black-backed, which has a uniform black back. There is only one possibility left, one bird that meets all the criteria:

Our bird must be a Three-toed Woodpecker.

Note that we have seen the bird for only a few seconds. The calculations required to identify it have taken longer, but this work has been done in our head and with the help of our field guide. Herein lies the key to rapid bird identification: extremely brief observation periods are all that is required for identification, *if you know what to look for and how to use what you see.*

Although it is possible to apply the three tests (location, characters of the family, and characters of the species) simultaneously, it is often helpful to follow a deductive order, from general to specific, as shown above. If at the end of the process we find ourselves with a complete mismatch — we think we have seen a purple woodpecker and find there isn't any in the book — we might have to backtrack and reconsider some of our choices. Perhaps it isn't a woodpecker at all. Or maybe we have eliminated a bird because of season or geography that should have been included. By knowing the order in which you made your identification decisions, you can most easily discover where you made your mistake.

Let us look at an example from a different part of the country — say, a suburb near Los Angeles, California, in spring. If we saw a small, greenish bird singing plaintively in a dense, broad-leaved shade tree, there would be literally a hundred possibilities. Our bird could be anything from a Lesser Goldfinch to one of several different flycatchers.

As in the woodpecker example, one of the first and most important steps would be to determine the correct family. Some clues would help us eliminate birds from consideration: perhaps the bird's posture is too horizontal to be a flycatcher; its bill isn't conical, like that of most finches and sparrows, or small and pointed, like that of a warbler; and its body is too small to be a thrush, tanager, oriole, or thrasher. Other clues would direct us toward a particular group of birds: the combination of a small, greenish gray bird with a relatively large head and a distinct, persistent song all suggest a vireo.

We might not be sure the bird is a vireo, but looking in our book we could begin serious comparisons based on this preliminary guess. Of the twelve vireos in North America, six or seven (the White-eyed, Red-eyed, Yellow-green, Black-capped, Yellow-throated, Philadelphia, and Black-whiskered) can be eliminated immediately, based on their range; if our field guide is marked for southern California, this will be very easy. The bird *could* be a Bell's Vireo, but that species is not very common in southern California. Also, the bird is probably not a Gray Vireo, which is too gray and prefers scrub-growth habitat.

But the remaining three choices — the Warbling Vireo, Solitary Vireo, and Hutton's Vireo — are all good possibilities. As we study the field guide, we might see that vocalization clues can be important. Hutton's Vireo has a nasal voice, unlike the musical song of our mystery bird; Hutton's Vireo is also more typically a bird of mixed woodlands (woods with conifers as well as deciduous trees). A good view of our bird reveals a fairly broad, whitish eyestripe and whitish underparts. The bird does not seem to have any wing bars — an important clue. This helps us eliminate Hutton's Vireo (which has two whitish wing bars) and the Solitary Vireo (which also has two), and further helps to rule out the uncommon Bell's Vireo (which usually has at

least one wingbar and has a very different song).
Our bird is probably the Warbling Vireo.

Careful reading of the species description for the
Warbling Vireo supports this choice. Its song, a
rambling warble, matches the description, as does
its typical habitat, general description, and overall
behavior. When you come down to a final choice,
and have found a species in the guide that seems to
meet all the criteria, you should feel confident that
you have identified the species correctly.

Indeed, finding the right match is one of the
added pleasures of birdwatching. It is a feeling akin
to the one you experience when you find the last
word in a crossword puzzle and it fits, making
sense in all directions; you know immediately that
you're right. You can then enjoy that special plea-
sure of real achievement: a challenge accepted and
a challenge met. It's a nice feeling.

PART II

BIRDING TIPS

❦ BIRDING TIPS ❦

The previous examples might still seem a little too easy to those who have had little success fumbling around with binoculars and field guides in the woods. It is bad enough to be a beginner, but worse to be a beginner who has tried, and failed, and must begin again.

Some of your difficulties might have little to do with the actual identification process. There are several problems that the beginner must overcome in order to become proficient in identification. Some are mechanical in nature and disappear with repeated practice. Others are simply tricks of the trade that you should learn as soon as possible.

Perhaps the simplest trick of all is to begin at the beginning. On your first few birding trips, concentrate on the most common species of your area and *take the time to learn them well.* Don't rush out on that first day and attempt to identify everything.

Instead, identify and then study, really study, your first few birds. The American Robin, for example, is well worth the effort, despite the tendency of beginners to dismiss it. Spend time getting to know it. Use your binoculars to observe the details of its streaked chin, its whitish eye-ring, the differences between the male, female, and immature. Become familiar with its posture and manner, the way it walks and the way it flies. You should learn enough about it that you could identify it anywhere, anytime, from any angle.

Realize that you are striving to establish a foundation of knowledge from which to tackle increasingly difficult problems. Knowing the Robin contributes more than just fluency with a single species. You'll know the attributes of an entire family, the thrushes, and be able to recognize whether or not a new bird is a member of the thrush family. You'll have a beginning point within the family that will help you learn the other members of the family. And most importantly, you'll know what isn't a thrush.

female

male

immature

A similar approach with the other common species of your area would reap enormous benefits. Learn just seven more birds — the Eastern or Western Kingbird, the Barn Swallow, the Red-eyed Vireo, the Red-winged Blackbird, the Yellow Warbler, the American Goldfinch, and the Chipping Sparrow — and you'll have an excellent guide to the

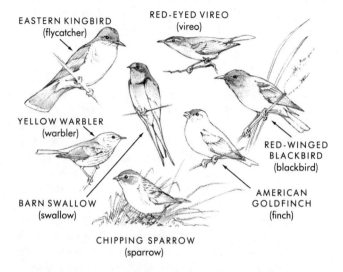

EASTERN KINGBIRD
(flycatcher)

RED-EYED VIREO
(vireo)

YELLOW WARBLER
(warbler)

RED-WINGED
BLACKBIRD
(blackbird)

BARN SWALLOW
(swallow)

AMERICAN
GOLDFINCH
(finch)

CHIPPING SPARROW
(sparrow)

North American bird families that provide the greatest difficulties and include most of the common species. If you can't find these particular birds in your area, another blackbird, sparrow, or whatever will do. The families you don't know yet can be recognized by the ways they differ from these common families. You'll be in position to tackle almost all of the songbirds.

In essence, you want to proceed step by step, confident of what you do know and aware of what you don't know. If a strange bird appears before you, you'll at least be able to analyze it knowledgeably. You will know what family it belongs to — or at least which families it *doesn't* belong to. You'll avoid that horrible confusion that can overcome beginners when they start in one direction, then another, trying to identify one mystery bird after another without ever coming to a satisfactory conclusion and ending up unsure of even a Robin when they see or hear it in the woods instead of on the front lawn.

1. Seeing:

Many beginners encounter great frustration when trying to see a small bird that is moving quickly through the brush, especially if they are accompanied by a more experienced birder who seems to be having no trouble observing the bird clearly. Some beginners react by cleaning their binoculars and making an appointment with their optometrist.

The truth is that the ability to see well in the field is less a function of the sharpness of your eyes than of experience and training. Most people have urban eyes used to the coarse motions of television shows, expressway traffic, and advertising hoopla. To become an efficient birdwatcher, you must literally relearn how to see. You must develop sensitivity to the slightest motion. You must master the ability to recognize the shape of a bird's head or body among the confusing lines of the foliage. Most importantly, you must teach your eyes to be aware of the possibilities.

There are some tricks that will speed your progress. When trying to see birds hidden within foliage, wait until you detect movement with your naked eye and then look at the general area with your binoculars in the hopes of being able to pinpoint the bird when it moves again.

Another trick is to check specific areas in the foliage according to your guess as to a bird's identity; if you hear a thrush-like call, check the tops of the

You have to train your eyes to look for birds, especially when they move quickly or are well camouflaged in good cover. Learn to spot birds with the naked eye as they move across the sky, in trees or bushes, or on the ground. As you become more familiar with the habits of birds, you will know which ones to expect in treetops or on power lines and which ones prefer the forest understory, fields, or woodland edges.

surrounding trees; if you suspect a woodpecker, scan the sides of the tree trunks; and so on.

The Audubon "squeakers" can be quite effective. These small wooden and metal devices produce strange, high-pitched noises that attract many birds out into the open where they can be easily viewed. Some birders can produce similar sounds by smacking their lips and have equal luck in drawing out shy birds. These techniques should be used with discretion, to avoid harassing the birds.

When trying to find a bird after hearing its song or call, be aware that many species are capable of an almost ventriloquistic effect, completely disguising their location. The acoustics of the forest interior can be especially deceptive, and it is easy to be misled and end up spending your time searching in the wrong direction.

Finally, recognize that some birds are such skulkers that it will take considerable patience and concerted efforts to finally see enough of them for identification. Persevere, keep your eyes alert, and you will be surprised how quickly you develop the knack of seeing birds in the wild.

2. Binoculars:

Seemingly a simple tool, binoculars actually take some time to learn how to use. Different makes and sizes vary in their optical quality, and all distort the appearance of birds to one extent or another. There is no solution to the problem other than purchasing a pair of quality binoculars and using them often enough so that you can become accustomed to their peculiarities.

Typical birding binoculars are 7×, 35, with center focusing and coated optics. The first number refers to the power of magnification; at 7× a bird 70 feet away would appear through the binoculars as if it were only 10 feet away. 6× is generally the lowest power suited for birding and some people prefer using 8×, 9×, or 10× for greater detail. Higher magnifications — 12× and especially 16× — are self-defeating, because most people cannot hold such powerful binoculars steady enough with their hands to avoid blurring the image. You then have to resort to bracing the binoculars on a tripod, tree, car roof, or some other stable base, which greatly limits your flexibility.

The second number — the 35 in 7×, 35 — refers to the diameter of the objective lens, which is important in determining the relative brightness of the image. The brighter the image, the easier it is to see details of the birds during low-light conditions, such as at dusk or when you are deep in the forest. For the same objective lens size, higher magnification binoculars produce relatively darker images; the lens arrangement necessary to increase magnification also increases light absorption and hence decreases the amount of light that passes through to your eye. Increasing the objective lens size increases brightness. My favorite binoculars are 7×, 42, as I generally feel the brightness and clarity of the image are more important than magnification.

Relative brightness can be calculated by dividing the objective lens size (e.g., 35 or 42) by the magnification (e.g., 7×). The result can be used to compare different binoculars. The higher the number you end up with, the brighter the image will appear. Thus the 7×, 42 binoculars (42 ÷ 7 = 6) will be brighter than the 7×, 35's.

Center focusing means that both tubes of the binoculars can be focused simultaneously by a single wheel on the main hinge. This feature is very important, given the need to focus quickly on a rapidly moving bird. On most binoculars the right barrel also focuses separately, to allow you to compensate for any difference in the strength of your eyes.

Coated optics are now almost standard in all but the cheapest binoculars. The coating on the lens and prisms greatly reduces unwanted reflections and thereby increases the relative brightness of the image.

All binoculars are a compromise between cost and quality, between size, magnification, and brightness. You should choose wisely; remember the points mentioned above, and if possible, borrow different pairs from friends so that you can try out different kinds in the field. Good binoculars are a major investment and can make a significant difference in how much you enjoy birding.

3. Colors:

The coloration of a bird varies according to the specific light conditions under which it is viewed. In part, this is due to the fact that the colors of bird feathers are a result of both pigments and the physical structure of the feathers.

The blue color of the Blue Jay, for example, is produced by an optical phenomenon that is similar to the one which produces the blue color of the sky. The internal cell structure of the feathers scatters blue light, while dark melanin pigments absorb other colors, permitting only the reflected blue light to appear. Some greens and most of the iridescent colors are caused by a similar interaction of pigments and cell structure. As a result, reflected light can make feathers appear a different color, so an observer can never be sure that the colors of a bird he sees will be exactly the same as those pictured in his field guide.

In addition, backlighting will often make a red bird appear gray, while frontlighting will make a dull bird appear bright. The male Indigo Bunting, for example, will appear brilliant blue with good frontlighting, but almost black if backlit, as when seen perched on a telephone line outlined by a bright sky.

backlighting
WHITE-WINGED
CROSSBILL

frontlighting
TREE SPARROW

filtered
sunlight
BLACK-
THROATED
BLUE WARBLER

Sunlight filtering through foliage will cast a green tint on birds. Iridescent plumages, such as those of the hummingbirds and some grackles, can look dramatically different depending on the light. Even specific tints can be distorted; the brilliant orange of a Northern Oriole can change from a reddish tint to yellowish when the background colors differ.

Such problems can be solved only by experience and by learning to compensate for differing light conditions. The beginner is advised to concentrate — just as experts do — on the *pattern* of colors rather than their specific shades. Although neophytes often look first for color, it is probably the single most misleading feature for identification.

4. Sizes:

The sizes of birds are frequently deceptive. What might be quite obviously a large or small bird when seen on your front lawn can appear completely different when seen in the varying conditions of fields, forests, or marshes.

For example, it is very hard to determine how large a soaring hawk is when you are not sure whether it is 200 or 600 feet in the air. Its proportions might give some indication of its bulk and thus its general size, but the combination of uncertain distance, hazy atmosphere, and the lack of nearby objects to provide a sense of scale can cause even experienced birders to be fooled. Flat estuaries and shorelines pose similar problems, because their great expanses tend to make distant objects appear closer than they actually are.

Further, songbirds flitting through the vegetation often appear smaller or larger depending on whether the foliage has large leaves or small leaves. A bird that looks large when standing among the small pebbles of a streambed can appear completely different when dwarfed by huge boulders. And binoculars in general distort your normal depth perception and corresponding sense of scale.

Be wary of exact measurements given in field guides and rely instead on a coarse judgment of

The same bird can look larger or smaller, depending on the scale of the leaves or other background features nearby.

whether the bird is the size of a sparrow, robin, pigeon, crow, eagle, or other familiar bird. Comparative measurements are more successful than absolute measurements. Like the clues provided by color, size clues often should be discounted when making your deliberations.

5. Hearing:

Learning to identify the songs and calls of the common birds is not as hard as it seems. The worst way to go about it is the hunt-and-peck method, whereby you hear a call and then try to track down its author; this can be very time-consuming.

A better way is to accompany an experienced birder on enough trips that his repeated identifications will enable you to remember the sounds; this is sometimes difficult, as it requires the cooperation of a second person.

The best method, and certainly the easiest, is to buy records or tapes of bird songs and listen to them regularly. The better albums have the bird calls arranged and keyed to a specific field guide.

When working with the records, concentrate on specific groups of birds, such as the vireos or flycatchers; it is often easier to learn the songs if you pay attention to the differences among several songs rather than the exact melody or tonality of any one song. And by working on one family at a time, you will learn the features that songs for each family have in common. This will enable you to tell whether you're listening to a thrush or a warbler, even if you can't tell *which* thrush or warbler is singing.

An excellent place to begin is with the songs of five similar brownish thrushes: the Gray-cheeked, Swainson's, Hermit, Veery, and Wood Thrush. The songs of all five are very similar, with clear, flutelike notes. But each has a peculiarity that enables you to recognize it easily. The Hermit's song, for example, begins with a characteristic long introductory note; the Swainson's song rises in pitch, while the Veery's descends; the Wood Thrush's song sometimes has guttural notes at the beginning and always finishes with a distinctive long note; and the Gray-cheeked's song has a sharp, abrupt ending.

This comparative technique can be applied to other groups of birds, so that you can quickly master the songs of the common species.

6. Abundance:

Beginners should realize that the populations of birds can be highly variable. Birds that are common across an entire state or region might be remarkably rare in your local area. Conversely, birds that are rare throughout the nation can be quite plentiful locally. Abundance is very hard to predict, and there is often no way to know other than by going out into the field and seeing which birds are there.

Bird populations can change within short time periods. Some seed-eating birds will suddenly concentrate in certain areas and then just as suddenly abandon them, depending on local availability of grain and seeds. The population levels of berry-feeding birds, such as Cedar Waxwings, can also fluctuate according to food resources.

Storms, unusual seasonal temperatures, or changing climatic conditions can affect both the numbers of any one species and the diversity of species found in a given area. Major alterations in habitat, such as those caused by man, almost always affect the local abundance of birds and the composition of populations.

Thus, you should be wary of general statements

Habitat changes—manmade or natural—have a direct impact on the abundance of birds in your area, and the types of species that are present. Monitoring these changes can be a fascinating hobby.

about the abundance of a species. In fact, an increasing number of field guides are beginning to drop abundance notations. Local area checklists, however, can be very useful, especially those prepared by birding groups such as the state chapters of the Audubon Society. You can modify the regional checklists at the end of this book to suit your needs by adding notes or highlighting certain birds that are common in your area, just as you can "personalize" your field guide.

Indeed, the changing populations of birds are one of the more fascinating features of birdwatching. In time, as you build your local area list and gain familiarity with the relative abundance of local species, you will begin to become aware of these seasonal and yearly changes. It can become an absorbing hobby to try to monitor these changes and understand the reasons for them.

7. Field Guides:

After working with many, many students, I feel that some field guides are more successful than others as introductory texts for the beginner.

In general, the field guides which feature accurate paintings are much easier to use by beginners than those which feature photographs. The photographic process introduces a number of distortions — color balance, prevailing light, altered perspective caused by telephoto lenses, the final printing process itself, etc. Theoretically a photograph might be superior, but in practice beginners have greater trouble correlating what they see in the field with the correct photograph.

Good drawings and paintings, on the other hand, are superior in their ability to accurately depict profile, posture, and the details of plumage. In my experience, such paintings are much easier for beginners to remember than a photograph. And, if the illustrations are done by a truly knowledgeable birder, they can include a slight emphasis on important characters, so that the diagnostic features are more prominent. Although this may involve a slight misrepresentation of a bird, it greatly helps beginners understand what they should look for when observing a particular species.

When buying a field guide, be sure to purchase the most current edition possible. Birds, and our knowledge of them, change constantly and it is important to have up-to-date information. Also, be sure to check which area the field guide covers; some books are specialized and are devoted to a single state, while others cover the entire country. Regional guides are perhaps the best compromise — they focus on fewer species and thus are simpler, yet they still offer sufficient coverage to be practical on short trips. Indeed, it's not a bad idea to buy several field guides to take advantage of the strong points of each.

8. Notebooks:

Most beginners don't appreciate the value of keeping a notebook until they actually begin to use one and discover how helpful it can be. Next to a good field guide, a notebook is the single most important tool in helping you learn the birds. The small time required to write down the name of each species as it is identified is well worth the effort. Among other things, a notebook:

- reminds you to check for and record information about the habitat, season, elevation, and location;

- provides space to record details of unidentified species which you can review later;

- builds a list of species for your local area, thereby helping you recognize rarities;

- helps you to be sure of your identifications by forcing you to record details of each bird as it is seen.

A good notebook should be a convenient size so that it can be easily carried with your field guide, and durable enough to withstand the rigors of field use. There should be space to record data about the location, to make lists of birds, and to draw sketches and take random notes. We have added pages to the back of this volume to provide a beginning notebook that will serve you through your initial stages of learning. Later, you can create your own notebook to meet your needs and interests.

Record for each outing:

1. Basic data: date, location, habitat.

2. List of birds identified, with notes about sex, behavior, special comments, etc.

3. Quick sketches of mystery birds, to note color pattern, size, shape. Later, back at home, you can take the time to research the bird in depth.

Finally, regardless of whether you are trying to learn the names of just a few birds that visit your feeder, or the names of every bird in your area, remember that the mental calculations are often more important than visual observations. Be comforted by the fact that even the experts have trouble at times — certain immature birds and birds in winter plumages confound even the most experienced birdwatchers. But with a little hard work, intelligently applied, most birds can be quickly and accurately identified.

PART III

CHECKLISTS

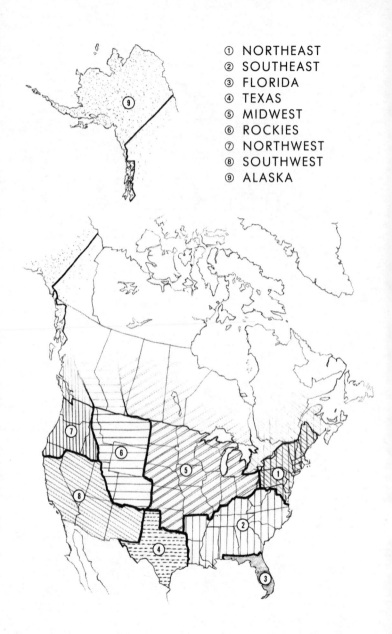

① NORTHEAST
② SOUTHEAST
③ FLORIDA
④ TEXAS
⑤ MIDWEST
⑥ ROCKIES
⑦ NORTHWEST
⑧ SOUTHWEST
⑨ ALASKA

❧ CHECKLISTS ❧

Checklists provide a list of the species found in a particular area and thereby allow you to eliminate some species from consideration while making sure you consider others. The following checklists have been annotated according to season and habitat, so that you will have this pertinent data available in one convenient place.

Most birds listed are quite common, at least at some time of year. A few uncommon birds of special interest are also included.

All checklists, though, are compromises. It is very hard to categorize birds in a definitive way because of their changing populations and ranges. In making up the following lists I was often plagued with inadequate data or, worse yet, faced with completely conflicting data. Often, it was impossible to make a satisfactory determination, and these lists should be used with a note of caution. Living creatures are by definition dynamic and variable. If you live near the boundaries of a region, be sure to check the checklist for the adjacent region.

I have divided the continental United States into nine areas (see map) for your convenience. (The northern areas extend into southern Canada.)

1. The **Northeast,** which includes all the New England states and the mid-Atlantic states from New York to Maryland.
2. The **Southeast,** from Virginia south to Georgia and Mississippi, and west to Arkansas and Louisiana.
3. **Florida.**
4. The **Midwest,** from Ohio west through the Great Plains to the eastern foothills of the Rockies and south to Oklahoma.
5. **Texas.**
6. The **Rockies,** from Idaho and Montana south to eastern Utah and Colorado, including all the mountainous portions of those states.
7. The **Northwest,** which includes the states of Washington, Oregon, northernmost California, and that portion of Idaho on the western foothills of the Rockies.
8. The **Southwest,** a large area from California east through Nevada and part of Utah and including the southern portion of the Rocky Mountains in Arizona and New Mexico.
9. **Alaska,** including the islands of the Aleutian chain.

In each list, the **season** column provides information about the seasonal status for each bird. A simple, four-letter code is used:

R = Resident, meaning the species is found somewhere within the region throughout the year. Bear in mind that climate varies so much within some regions that a bird can be a summer visitor to one section of the region and be confined to a different section during the winter; the bird would then be a resident for the region as a whole, although it is present in only portions of the region at any one time. This is especially true for the Southeast and Southwest regions.

B = **Breeding,** meaning the bird is only a summer resident of the region where it breeds; it leaves the region during the fall and winter, but may be seen migrating into or out of the area during spring and fall.

W = **Winter,** meaning the bird is a winter visitor and spends at least a portion of the winter months residing in the region.

M = **Migrant,** meaning the bird migrates through the region. Usually the bird will be migrating enroute to either a breeding or wintering area, but some birds, such as oceanic ones, do not travel in a consistent direction. Their travels can be part of a general dispersal across vast areas, as is typical of immature birds.

Finally, the last twelve columns in each list provide information about **habitat.** These assignments are certainly the most difficult to make. On one hand, a heavy storm can force a bird out of its normal habitat and range; under these special conditions it might be found literally anywhere. On the other hand, most birds show a definite preference for particular habitat types and it is extremely helpful to know their predilections. Further, in one region, or perhaps even a portion of a region, a species might occupy habitats it ignores elsewhere. In the end, I tried to make conservative choices and be inclusive rather than exclusive. Habitats where the bird appears during migration are usually given, as well as those where it breeds or spends the winter.

The twelve habitats are as follows:

OCEAN = Offshore waters of the ocean, often far out to sea.

SHORE = Seashore itself, including the waters visible from land, sandy beaches, and nearby dune areas. Also includes shores of the Great Lakes.

SALT = Saltwater marshes, lagoons, bays, and estuaries, sometimes extending inland as far as salt or brackish water persists.

FRESH = Freshwater lakes, ponds, rivers, streams, marshes, and swamps; wherever the vegetation type is dominated by the influence of fresh water.

GRASS = Prairies, grasslands, alpine meadows, and even tundra; wherever grass and short shrubs typify the landscape.

DESERTS = Sagebrush and cactus country where arid conditions prevail.

SCRUB = Scrub growth, dense thickets, and bushes; often a very limited habitat type bordering forests or woodlands.

O WOODS = Open woods; woodlands where the trees are spread out and there is no contiguous canopy.

D WOODS = Deciduous woods; forests dominated by broad-leaved deciduous trees.

C WOODS = Coniferous woods; forests dominated by conifers such as spruce, fir, and pine.

FARMS = Farms; cultivated lands, including pastures, crop fields, hedgerows, orchards, and other agricultural lands.

TOWNS = Towns, including the inner cities, city parks, suburbs, gardens, and places where manmade structures dominate.

An **X** indicates a species is found in that habitat.

CHECKLIST OF NORTHEASTERN BIRDS

	SEASON	OCEAN	SHORE	SALT	FRESH	GRASS	DESERT	SCRUB	O WOODS	D WOODS	C WOODS	FARMS	TOWNS
LOONS													
Common Loon	R	X	X	X	X								
Red-throated Loon	W		X	X	X								
GREBES													
Red-necked Grebe	W		X	X	X								
Horned Grebe	W		X	X	X								
Pied-billed Grebe	R		X	X	X								
SHEARWATERS													
Sooty Shearwater	M	X											
STORM-PETRELS													
Wilson's Storm-petrel	M	X	X	X									
BOOBIES & GANNETS													
Northern Gannet	W	X	X	X									

	SEASON	OCEAN	SHORE	SALT	FRESH	GRASS	DESERT	SCRUB	O WOODS	D WOODS	C WOODS	FARMS	TOWNS

CORMORANTS

	SEASON	OCEAN	SHORE	SALT	FRESH	GRASS	DESERT	SCRUB	O WOODS	D WOODS	C WOODS	FARMS	TOWNS
Great Cormorant	W		X	X									
Double-crested Cormorant	R		X	X	X								

HERONS & BITTERNS

	SEASON	OCEAN	SHORE	SALT	FRESH	GRASS	DESERT	SCRUB	O WOODS	D WOODS	C WOODS	FARMS	TOWNS
Great Blue Heron	R			X	X								
Green-backed Heron	B			X	X								
Little Blue Heron	R			X	X								
Cattle Egret	R			X	X	X						X	
Tricolored Heron	R			X									
Great Egret	R			X	X								
Snowy Egret	R			X	X								
Black-crowned Night-heron	R			X	X								
Yellow-crowned Night-heron	B			X	X								
American Bittern	B			X	X								
Least Bittern	B				X								

IBISES

	SEASON	OCEAN	SHORE	SALT	FRESH	GRASS	DESERT	SCRUB	O WOODS	D WOODS	C WOODS	FARMS	TOWNS
Glossy Ibis	B			X	X								

SWANS

	SEASON	OCEAN	SHORE	SALT	FRESH	GRASS	DESERT	SCRUB	O WOODS	D WOODS	C WOODS	FARMS	TOWNS
Mute Swan	R			X	X	X							X
Tundra Swan	W			X	X	X							

	SEASON	OCEAN	SHORE	SALT	FRESH	GRASS	DESERT	SCRUB	O WOODS	D WOODS	C WOODS	FARMS	TOWNS

GEESE

	SEASON	OCEAN	SHORE	SALT	FRESH	GRASS	DESERT	SCRUB	O WOODS	D WOODS	C WOODS	FARMS	TOWNS
Canada Goose	R			X	X	X						X	
Brant	W	X	X										
Snow Goose	W			X	X	X	X						

MARSH DUCKS

	SEASON	OCEAN	SHORE	SALT	FRESH	GRASS	DESERT	SCRUB	O WOODS	D WOODS	C WOODS	FARMS	TOWNS
Mallard	R			X	X	X							
Black Duck	R			X	X	X							
Pintail	R			X	X	X							
Gadwall	R			X	X	X							
American Wigeon	R			X	X	X							
Northern Shoveler	R			X	X								
Blue-winged Teal	B			X	X	X							
Green-winged Teal	R			X	X								
Wood Duck	R				X								

DIVING DUCKS

	SEASON	OCEAN	SHORE	SALT	FRESH	GRASS	DESERT	SCRUB	O WOODS	D WOODS	C WOODS	FARMS	TOWNS
Redhead	R			X	X								
Canvasback	W			X	X								
Ring-necked Duck	R			X	X								
Greater Scaup	W		X	X	X								
Lesser Scaup	W		X	X	X								
Common Goldeneye	R		X	X	X								
Bufflehead	W		X	X	X								
Harlequin Duck	W		X	X									
Common Eider	R		X	X									
King Eider	W		X	X	X								
Oldsquaw	W	X	X	X	X								
Black Scoter	W	X	X	X									
White-winged Scoter	W		X	X									
Surf Scoter	W	X	X	X									

STIFF-TAILED DUCKS

	SEASON	OCEAN	SHORE	SALT	FRESH	GRASS	DESERT	SCRUB	O WOODS	D WOODS	C WOODS	FARMS	TOWNS
Ruddy Duck	R		X	X	X								

MERGANSERS

	SEASON	OCEAN	SHORE	SALT	FRESH	GRASS	DESERT	SCRUB	O WOODS	D WOODS	C WOODS	FARMS	TOWNS
Common Merganser	R			X	X								
Red-breasted Merganser	R		X	X	X								
Hooded Merganser	R			X	X								

VULTURES

	SEASON	OCEAN	SHORE	SALT	FRESH	GRASS	DESERT	SCRUB	O WOODS	D WOODS	C WOODS	FARMS	TOWNS
Turkey Vulture	R					X		X				X	
Black Vulture	R					X		X				X	

ACCIPITERS

	SEASON	OCEAN	SHORE	SALT	FRESH	GRASS	DESERT	SCRUB	O WOODS	D WOODS	C WOODS	FARMS	TOWNS
Goshawk	R								X	X	X	X	
Cooper's Hawk	R								X	X	X	X	
Sharp-shinned Hawk	R									X	X	X	

HARRIERS

	SEASON	OCEAN	SHORE	SALT	FRESH	GRASS	DESERT	SCRUB	O WOODS	D WOODS	C WOODS	FARMS	TOWNS
Northern Harrier	R			X	X	X						X	

BUTEOS

	SEASON	OCEAN	SHORE	SALT	FRESH	GRASS	DESERT	SCRUB	O WOODS	D WOODS	C WOODS	FARMS	TOWNS
Rough-legged Hawk	W		X	X	X	X						X	
Red-tailed Hawk	R			X	X			X	X	X		X	
Red-shouldered Hawk	R				X			X	X	X	X	X	
Broad-winged Hawk	B				X				X	X	X	X	

	SEASON	OCEAN	SHORE	SALT	FRESH	GRASS	DESERT	SCRUB	O WOODS	D WOODS	C WOODS	FARMS	TOWNS

EAGLES

	SEASON	OCEAN	SHORE	SALT	FRESH	GRASS	DESERT	SCRUB	O WOODS	D WOODS	C WOODS	FARMS	TOWNS
Bald Eagle	R		X	X	X								

OSPREY

	SEASON	OCEAN	SHORE	SALT	FRESH	GRASS	DESERT	SCRUB	O WOODS	D WOODS	C WOODS	FARMS	TOWNS
Osprey	B		X	X	X								

FALCONS

	SEASON	OCEAN	SHORE	SALT	FRESH	GRASS	DESERT	SCRUB	O WOODS	D WOODS	C WOODS	FARMS	TOWNS
Peregrine Falcon	R	X		X	X								X
Merlin	M	X			X						X	X	
American Kestrel	R				X		X	X				X	X

GROUSE

	SEASON	OCEAN	SHORE	SALT	FRESH	GRASS	DESERT	SCRUB	O WOODS	D WOODS	C WOODS	FARMS	TOWNS
Spruce Grouse	R							X			X		
Ruffed Grouse	R							X	X	X	X	X	

QUAIL & PHEASANTS

	SEASON	OCEAN	SHORE	SALT	FRESH	GRASS	DESERT	SCRUB	O WOODS	D WOODS	C WOODS	FARMS	TOWNS
Bobwhite	R					X	X	X				X	
Ring-necked Pheasant	R					X		X				X	

TURKEYS

	SEASON	OCEAN	SHORE	SALT	FRESH	GRASS	DESERT	SCRUB	O WOODS	D WOODS	C WOODS	FARMS	TOWNS
Wild Turkey	R								X	X	X	X	

	SEASON	OCEAN	SHORE	SALT	FRESH	GRASS	DESERT	SCRUB	O WOODS	D WOODS	C WOODS	FARMS	TOWNS

RAILS

	SEASON	OCEAN	SHORE	SALT	FRESH	GRASS	DESERT	SCRUB	O WOODS	D WOODS	C WOODS	FARMS	TOWNS
King Rail	R			X	X								
Clapper Rail	R			X									
Virginia Rail	R			X	X								
Sora	B			X	X								X
Common Gallinule (Moorhen)	B				X								
American Coot	R			X	X								X

OYSTERCATCHERS

	SEASON	OCEAN	SHORE	SALT	FRESH	GRASS	DESERT	SCRUB	O WOODS	D WOODS	C WOODS	FARMS	TOWNS
American Oystercatcher	B	C		X	X								

PLOVERS

	SEASON	OCEAN	SHORE	SALT	FRESH	GRASS	DESERT	SCRUB	O WOODS	D WOODS	C WOODS	FARMS	TOWNS
Semipalmated Plover	M		X	X	X								
Killdeer	R		X	X	X	X							X
Piping Plover	B		X	X									
Lesser Golden Plover	M		X	X	X	X							X
Black-bellied Plover	W		X	X	X	X							X

GODWITS

	SEASON	OCEAN	SHORE	SALT	FRESH	GRASS	DESERT	SCRUB	O WOODS	D WOODS	C WOODS	FARMS	TOWNS
Hudsonian Godwit	M			X	X	X	X						

CURLEWS

	SEASON	OCEAN	SHORE	SALT	FRESH	GRASS	DESERT	SCRUB	O WOODS	D WOODS	C WOODS	FARMS	TOWNS
Whimbrel	M			X	X	X	X						

	SEASON	OCEAN	SHORE	SALT	FRESH	GRASS	DESERT	SCRUB	O WOODS	D WOODS	C WOODS	FARMS	TOWNS

UPLAND SANDPIPERS

	SEASON	OCEAN	SHORE	SALT	FRESH	GRASS	DESERT	SCRUB	O WOODS	D WOODS	C WOODS	FARMS	TOWNS
Upland Sandpiper	B					X						X	
Solitary Sandpiper	M				X								
Spotted Sandpiper	B		X	X	X	X							
Willet	R		X	X	X								
Greater Yellowlegs	M			X	X	X							
Lesser Yellowlegs	M		X	X	X	X							

WOODCOCK

	SEASON	OCEAN	SHORE	SALT	FRESH	GRASS	DESERT	SCRUB	O WOODS	D WOODS	C WOODS	FARMS	TOWNS
American Woodcock	R								X	X	X	X	

SNIPE

	SEASON	OCEAN	SHORE	SALT	FRESH	GRASS	DESERT	SCRUB	O WOODS	D WOODS	C WOODS	FARMS	TOWNS
Common Snipe	R			X	X	X							X

SANDPIPERS

	SEASON	OCEAN	SHORE	SALT	FRESH	GRASS	DESERT	SCRUB	O WOODS	D WOODS	C WOODS	FARMS	TOWNS
Short-billed Dowitcher	M		X	X	X								
Long-billed Dowitcher	M		X	X	X								
Red Knot	M		X	X									
Sanderling	W		X	X									
Semipalmated Sandpiper	M		X	X	X								
Western Sandpiper	M		X	X	X								
Least Sandpiper	M		X	X	X								

SANDPIPERS, *continued*

	SEASON	OCEAN	SHORE	SALT	FRESH	GRASS	DESERT	SCRUB	O WOODS	D WOODS	C WOODS	FARMS	TOWNS
Ruddy Turnstone	W		X	X									
Purple Sandpiper	W		X	X									
Dunlin	W		X	X	X								

GULLS

	SEASON	OCEAN	SHORE	SALT	FRESH	GRASS	DESERT	SCRUB	O WOODS	D WOODS	C WOODS	FARMS	TOWNS
Glaucous Gull	W		X	X	X								X
Iceland Gull	W		X	X	X								X
Great Black-backed Gull	R		X	X	X								X
Herring Gull	R		X	X	X	X						X	X
Ring-billed Gull	R		X	X	X	X						X	X
Laughing Gull	B		X	X	X	X						X	X
Bonaparte's Gull	W		X	X	X								X
Black-legged Kittiwake	W	X	X										

TERNS

	SEASON	OCEAN	SHORE	SALT	FRESH	GRASS	DESERT	SCRUB	O WOODS	D WOODS	C WOODS	FARMS	TOWNS
Forster's Tern	B			X	X								
Common Tern	B		X	X	X								
Arctic Tern	M	X	X	X									
Least Tern	B		X	X	X								
Caspian Tern	B		X	X	X								
Black Tern	B		X	X	X							X	

SKIMMERS

	SEASON	OCEAN	SHORE	SALT	FRESH	GRASS	DESERT	SCRUB	O WOODS	D WOODS	C WOODS	FARMS	TOWNS
Black Skimmer	B		X	X									

ALCIDS

	SEASON	OCEAN	SHORE	SALT	FRESH	GRASS	DESERT	SCRUB	O WOODS	D WOODS	C WOODS	FARMS	TOWNS
Razorbill	R	X	X										

	SEASON	OCEAN	SHORE	SALT	FRESH	GRASS	DESERT	SCRUB	O WOODS	D WOODS	C WOODS	FARMS	TOWNS

ALCIDS, *continued*

	SEASON	OCEAN	SHORE	SALT	FRESH	GRASS	DESERT	SCRUB	O WOODS	D WOODS	C WOODS	FARMS	TOWNS
Common Murre	W	X	X										
Thick-billed Murre	W	X	X										
Dovekie	W	X	X										
Black Guillemot	R	X	X										
Atlantic Puffin	R	X	X										

PIGEONS & DOVES

	SEASON	OCEAN	SHORE	SALT	FRESH	GRASS	DESERT	SCRUB	O WOODS	D WOODS	C WOODS	FARMS	TOWNS
Rock Dove	R											X	X
Mourning Dove	R					X		X				X	X

CUCKOOS

	SEASON	OCEAN	SHORE	SALT	FRESH	GRASS	DESERT	SCRUB	O WOODS	D WOODS	C WOODS	FARMS	TOWNS
Yellow-billed Cuckoo	B								X	X	X	X	
Black-billed Cuckoo	B							X	X	X	X	X	

OWLS

	SEASON	OCEAN	SHORE	SALT	FRESH	GRASS	DESERT	SCRUB	O WOODS	D WOODS	C WOODS	FARMS	TOWNS
Barn Owl	R					X		X	X			X	X
Eastern Screech Owl	R								X	X		X	X
Great Horned Owl	R							X	X	X	X	X	X
Snowy Owl	W	X	X	X	X								
Barred Owl	R				X				X	X	X	X	
Long-eared Owl	R								X	X	X	X	X
Short-eared Owl	R			X	X	X		X				X	
Saw-whet Owl	R								X	X	X		X

GOATSUCKERS

	SEASON	OCEAN	SHORE	SALT	FRESH	GRASS	DESERT	SCRUB	O WOODS	D WOODS	C WOODS	FARMS	TOWNS
Chuck-will's-widow	B								X	X	X	X	
Whip-poor-will	B								X	X	X	X	
Common Nighthawk	B					X			X			X	X

	SEASON	OCEAN	SHORE	SALT	FRESH	GRASS	DESERT	SCRUB	O WOODS	D WOODS	C WOODS	FARMS	TOWNS
SWIFTS													
Chimney Swift	B								X			X	X
HUMMINGBIRDS													
Ruby-throated Hummingbird	B								X	X	X	X	X
KINGFISHERS													
Belted Kingfisher	R		X	X	X								
WOODPECKERS													
Common Flicker	R					X		X	X	X	X	X	X
Pileated Woodpecker	R								X	X			
Red-bellied Woodpecker	R							X	X	X	X	X	X
Red-headed Woodpecker	R				X			X	X			X	X
Yellow-bellied Sapsucker	R								X	X	X	X	X
Hairy Woodpecker	R								X	X	X	X	X
Downy Woodpecker	R								X	X	X	X	X
Three-toed Woodpecker	R								X	X			
Black-backed Woodpecker	R								X		X		
FLYCATCHERS													
Eastern Kingbird	B					X		X	X			X	X
Great Crested Flycatcher	B							X	X	X	X	X	X
Eastern Phoebe	R							X	X	X		X	X
Yellow-bellied Flycatcher	B							X	X		X		

FLYCATCHERS, continued

	SEASON	OCEAN	SHORE	SALT	FRESH	GRASS	DESERT	SCRUB	O WOODS	D WOODS	C WOODS	FARMS	TOWNS
Acadian Flycatcher	B								X	X	X	X	
Alder Flycatcher	B							X	X	X			
Willow Flycatcher	B							X	X	X			
Least Flycatcher	B							X	X	X		X	X
Eastern Wood Pewee	B							X	X	X	X	X	X
Olive-sided Flycatcher	B							X	X		X	X	

LARKS

	SEASON	OCEAN	SHORE	SALT	FRESH	GRASS	DESERT	SCRUB	O WOODS	D WOODS	C WOODS	FARMS	TOWNS
Horned Lark	R		X			X						X	X

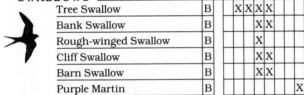

SWALLOWS

	SEASON	OCEAN	SHORE	SALT	FRESH	GRASS	DESERT	SCRUB	O WOODS	D WOODS	C WOODS	FARMS	TOWNS
Tree Swallow	B		X	X	X	X						X	X
Bank Swallow	B				X	X						X	X
Rough-winged Swallow	B				X							X	X
Cliff Swallow	B				X	X						X	X
Barn Swallow	B				X	X						X	X
Purple Martin	B									X		X	X

JAYS & CROWS

	SEASON	OCEAN	SHORE	SALT	FRESH	GRASS	DESERT	SCRUB	O WOODS	D WOODS	C WOODS	FARMS	TOWNS
Blue Jay	R								X	X	X	X	X
Common Raven	R		X		X	X		X	X	X	X	X	
Common Crow	R					X		X	X	X		X	X
Fish Crow	R		X	X	X								

TITMICE

	SEASON	OCEAN	SHORE	SALT	FRESH	GRASS	DESERT	SCRUB	O WOODS	D WOODS	C WOODS	FARMS	TOWNS
Black-capped Chickadee	R							X	X	X	X	X	X
Carolina Chickadee	R								X	X		X	X
Tufted Titmouse	R								X	X		X	X

	SEASON	OCEAN	SHORE	SALT	FRESH	GRASS	DESERT	SCRUB	O WOODS	D WOODS	C WOODS	FARMS	TOWNS

NUTHATCHES

	SEASON	OCEAN	SHORE	SALT	FRESH	GRASS	DESERT	SCRUB	O WOODS	D WOODS	C WOODS	FARMS	TOWNS
White-breasted Nuthatch	R								X	X	X	X	X
Red-breasted Nuthatch	R								X	X	X		

CREEPERS

	SEASON	OCEAN	SHORE	SALT	FRESH	GRASS	DESERT	SCRUB	O WOODS	D WOODS	C WOODS	FARMS	TOWNS
Brown Creeper	R								X	X			

WRENS

	SEASON	OCEAN	SHORE	SALT	FRESH	GRASS	DESERT	SCRUB	O WOODS	D WOODS	C WOODS	FARMS	TOWNS
House Wren	B							X	X			X	X
Winter Wren	R							X	X	X	X		X
Carolina Wren	R							X	X		X	X	X
Marsh Wren	R				X								
Sedge Wren	B			X	X								

THRASHERS

	SEASON	OCEAN	SHORE	SALT	FRESH	GRASS	DESERT	SCRUB	O WOODS	D WOODS	C WOODS	FARMS	TOWNS
Mockingbird	R							X	X			X	X
Catbird	R							X	X	X		X	X
Brown Thrasher	R							X	X			X	X

THRUSHES

	SEASON	OCEAN	SHORE	SALT	FRESH	GRASS	DESERT	SCRUB	O WOODS	D WOODS	C WOODS	FARMS	TOWNS
American Robin	R							X	X	X		X	X
Wood Thrush	B								X	X			
Hermit Thrush	R								X	X	X		
Swainson's Thrush	B								X	X	X		
Gray-cheeked Thrush	B								X	X	X		
Veery	B							X	X	X			
Eastern Bluebird	R						X		X			X	X
Blue-gray Gnatcatcher	B							X	X	X			
Golden-crowned Kinglet	R										X		
Ruby-crowned Kinglet	R							X	X	X	X		

	SEASON	OCEAN	SHORE	SALT	FRESH	GRASS	DESERT	SCRUB	O WOODS	D WOODS	C WOODS	FARMS	TOWNS
PIPITS													
Water Pipit	W		X		X							X	X
WAXWINGS													
Cedar Waxwing	R							X	X	X	X	X	X
SHRIKES													
Loggerhead Shrike	B					X		X	X			X	
STARLINGS													
Starling	R											X	X
VIREOS													
Solitary Vireo	B								X	X			
White-eyed Vireo	B							X				X	
Yellow-throated Vireo	B								X	X		X	X
Red-eyed Vireo	B								X	X		X	X
Philadelphia Vireo	B							X	X			X	
Warbling Vireo	B								X	X		X	X
WARBLERS													
Black-and-white Warbler	B								X	X			
Prothonotary Warbler	B				X				X	X			
Worm-eating Warbler	B							X	X	X			
Golden-winged Warbler	B							X	X			X	
Blue-winged Warbler	B							X	X			X	
Tennessee Warbler	B							X	X	X	X		

WARBLERS, continued

Nashville Warbler	B							X	X	X	X		
Northern Parula	B				X			X	X	X	X	X	
Yellow Warbler	B				X			X	X			X	
Magnolia Warbler	B							X	X	X	X		
Cape May Warbler	B								X	X	X		
Yellow-rumped Warbler	R							X	X	X	X		
Black-throated Green Warbler	B								X	X	X		
Black-throated Blue Warbler	B							X	X	X	X		
Cerulean Warbler	B								X	X			
Blackburnian Warbler	B								X	X	X		
Chestnut-sided Warbler	B							X	X	X		X	
Bay-breasted Warbler	B								X	X	X		
Blackpoll Warbler	B								X	X	X		
Pine Warbler	B										X		
Prairie Warbler	B							X	X	X	X		
Palm Warbler	B				X	X		X				X	
Ovenbird	B								X	X	X		
Northern Waterthrush	B		X						X	X	X		
Common Yellowthroat	R							X	X			X	
Yellow-breasted Chat	B							X					
Kentucky Warbler	B								X	X			
Mourning Warbler	B							X		X			
Hooded Warbler	B									X			
Wilson's Warbler	B							X	X	X			
Canada Warbler	B							X	X	X	X		
American Redstart	B							X	X	X			

WEAVER FINCHES

| House Sparrow | R | | | | | | | | | | | X | X |

BLACKBIRDS

	SEASON	OCEAN	SHORE	SALT	FRESH	GRASS	DESERT	SCRUB	O WOODS	D WOODS	C WOODS	FARMS	TOWNS
Bobolink	B				X	X						X	
Eastern Meadowlark	R					X						X	
Red-winged Blackbird	R			X	X	X						X	
Orchard Oriole	B								X			X	X
Northern Oriole	B								X	X		X	X
Rusty Blackbird	R				X				X	X	X		
Common Grackle	R								X			X	X
Brown-headed Cowbird	R								X			X	X

TANAGERS

	SEASON	OCEAN	SHORE	SALT	FRESH	GRASS	DESERT	SCRUB	O WOODS	D WOODS	C WOODS	FARMS	TOWNS
Scarlet Tanager	B								X	X			

CARDINALS & BUNTINGS

	SEASON	OCEAN	SHORE	SALT	FRESH	GRASS	DESERT	SCRUB	O WOODS	D WOODS	C WOODS	FARMS	TOWNS
Cardinal	R								X	X		X	X
Rose-breasted Grosbeak	B								X	X	X	X	X
Blue Grosbeak	B								X			X	
Indigo Bunting	B								X	X		X	

FINCHES

	SEASON	OCEAN	SHORE	SALT	FRESH	GRASS	DESERT	SCRUB	O WOODS	D WOODS	C WOODS	FARMS	TOWNS
Evening Grosbeak	R								X	X	X	X	X
Purple Finch	R									X	X	X	X
House Finch	R						X	X				X	X
Pine Siskin	R								X	X			
American Goldfinch	R					X		X				X	X
Red Crossbill	R										X		
White-winged Crossbill	W										X		

	SEASON	OCEAN	SHORE	SALT	FRESH	GRASS	DESERT	SCRUB	O WOODS	D WOODS	C WOODS	FARMS	TOWNS
Rufous-sided Towhee	R							X	X			X	X
Savannah Sparrow	B		X	X		X						X	
Seaside Sparrow	B		X	X				X					
Vesper Sparrow	R		X			X		X				X	
Dark-eyed Junco	R								X	X	X	X	X
Tree Sparrow	W		X	X	X	X		X	X			X	X
Chipping Sparrow	B					X		X	X			X	X
Field Sparrow	R					X		X				X	
White-crowned Sparrow	M					X		X	X			X	X
White-throated Sparrow	R							X	X	X	X	X	X
Fox Sparrow	W							X		X	X	X	
Swamp Sparrow	R			X	X			X	X			X	
Song Sparrow	R		X	X	X			X	X	X		X	X
Lapland Longspur	W		X	X	X	X						X	X
Snow Bunting	W		X			X		X				X	

CHECKLIST OF SOUTHEASTERN BIRDS

	SEASON	OCEAN	SHORE	SALT	FRESH	GRASS	DESERT	SCRUB	O WOODS	D WOODS	C WOODS	FARMS	TOWNS
LOONS													
Common Loon	W		X	X	X								
Red-throated Loon	W		X	X	X								
GREBES													
Red-necked Grebe	W		X	X	X								
Horned Grebe	W		X	X	X								
Pied-billed Grebe	R		X	X	X								
SHEARWATERS													
Cory's Shearwater	M	X											
Greater Shearwater	M	X											
Audubon's Shearwater	M	X											
Sooty Shearwater	M	X											
STORM-PETRELS													
Wilson's Storm-petrel	M	X	X	X									
PELICANS													
Brown Pelican	R	X	X	X									
White Pelican	W		X	X	X								

BOOBIES & GANNETS

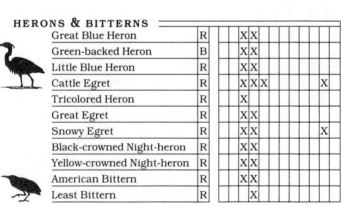

	SEASON	OCEAN	SHORE	SALT	FRESH	GRASS	DESERT	SCRUB	O WOODS	D WOODS	C WOODS	FARMS	TOWNS
Northern Gannet	W	X	X	X									

CORMORANTS

	SEASON	OCEAN	SHORE	SALT	FRESH	GRASS	DESERT	SCRUB	O WOODS	D WOODS	C WOODS	FARMS	TOWNS
Double-crested Cormorant	R		X	X	X								
Olivaceous Cormorant	R		X	X	X								

ANHINGAS

	SEASON	OCEAN	SHORE	SALT	FRESH	GRASS	DESERT	SCRUB	O WOODS	D WOODS	C WOODS	FARMS	TOWNS
Anhinga	R			X	X								

HERONS & BITTERNS

	SEASON	OCEAN	SHORE	SALT	FRESH	GRASS	DESERT	SCRUB	O WOODS	D WOODS	C WOODS	FARMS	TOWNS
Great Blue Heron	R			X	X								
Green-backed Heron	B			X	X								
Little Blue Heron	R			X	X								
Cattle Egret	R			X	X	X						X	
Tricolored Heron	R			X									
Great Egret	R			X	X								
Snowy Egret	R			X	X							X	
Black-crowned Night-heron	R			X	X								
Yellow-crowned Night-heron	R			X	X								
American Bittern	R			X	X								
Least Bittern	R				X								

	SEASON	OCEAN	SHORE	SALT	FRESH	GRASS	DESERT	SCRUB	O WOODS	D WOODS	C WOODS	FARMS	TOWNS
STORKS													
Wood Stork	R		X	X	X								
IBISES													
White-faced Ibis	R			X	X								
Glossy Ibis	R			X	X								
White Ibis	R			X	X								
SWANS													
Tundra Swan	W		X	X	X								
GEESE													
Canada Goose	W			X	X	X						X	
Brant	W	X	X										
White-fronted Goose	W				X	X							
Snow Goose	W	X	X	X	X								
MARSH DUCKS													
Mallard	W			X	X	X							
Black Duck	W			X	X								
Mottled Duck	R		X	X	X								
Pintail	W			X	X								
Gadwall	W			X	X	X							
American Wigeon	W			X	X	X							
Northern Shoveler	W			X	X								
Blue-winged Teal	W			X	X	X							

MARSH DUCKS, continued

	SEASON	OCEAN	SHORE	SALT	FRESH	GRASS	DESERT	SCRUB	O WOODS	D WOODS	C WOODS	FARMS	TOWNS
Green-winged Teal	W			X	X								
Wood Duck	R				X								

WHISTLING DUCKS
	SEASON	OCEAN	SHORE	SALT	FRESH	GRASS	DESERT	SCRUB	O WOODS	D WOODS	C WOODS	FARMS	TOWNS
Fulvous Whistling Duck	R				X	X						X	

DIVING DUCKS
	SEASON	OCEAN	SHORE	SALT	FRESH	GRASS	DESERT	SCRUB	O WOODS	D WOODS	C WOODS	FARMS	TOWNS
Redhead	W			X	X								
Canvasback	W			X	X								
Ring-necked Duck	W			X	X								
Greater Scaup	W		X	X	X								
Lesser Scaup	W		X	X	X								
Common Goldeneye	W		X	X	X								
Bufflehead	W		X	X	X								

STIFF-TAILED DUCKS
	SEASON	OCEAN	SHORE	SALT	FRESH	GRASS	DESERT	SCRUB	O WOODS	D WOODS	C WOODS	FARMS	TOWNS
Ruddy Duck	W			X	X								

MERGANSERS
	SEASON	OCEAN	SHORE	SALT	FRESH	GRASS	DESERT	SCRUB	O WOODS	D WOODS	C WOODS	FARMS	TOWNS
Common Merganser	W			X	X								
Red-breasted Merganser	W		X	X	X								
Hooded Merganser	R			X	X								

VULTURES
	SEASON	OCEAN	SHORE	SALT	FRESH	GRASS	DESERT	SCRUB	O WOODS	D WOODS	C WOODS	FARMS	TOWNS
Turkey Vulture	R					X		X		X		X	
Black Vulture	R					X		X		X		X	

	SEASON	OCEAN	SHORE	SALT	FRESH	GRASS	DESERT	SCRUB	O WOODS	D WOODS	C WOODS	FARMS	TOWNS

KITES

	SEASON	OCEAN	SHORE	SALT	FRESH	GRASS	DESERT	SCRUB	O WOODS	D WOODS	C WOODS	FARMS	TOWNS
Mississippi Kite	B							X	X	X			
Swallow-tailed Kite	B				X			X	X				

ACCIPITERS

	SEASON	OCEAN	SHORE	SALT	FRESH	GRASS	DESERT	SCRUB	O WOODS	D WOODS	C WOODS	FARMS	TOWNS
Cooper's Hawk	R								X	X	X	X	
Sharp-shinned Hawk	R								X	X	X		

HARRIERS

	SEASON	OCEAN	SHORE	SALT	FRESH	GRASS	DESERT	SCRUB	O WOODS	D WOODS	C WOODS	FARMS	TOWNS
Northern Harrier	W				X	X							

BUTEOS

	SEASON	OCEAN	SHORE	SALT	FRESH	GRASS	DESERT	SCRUB	O WOODS	D WOODS	C WOODS	FARMS	TOWNS
Rough-legged Hawk	W					X						X	
Red-tailed Hawk	R					X		X	X	X		X	
Red-shouldered Hawk	R					X			X	X		X	
Broad-winged Hawk	B					X			X	X			

EAGLES

	SEASON	OCEAN	SHORE	SALT	FRESH	GRASS	DESERT	SCRUB	O WOODS	D WOODS	C WOODS	FARMS	TOWNS
Bald Eagle	R		X	X	X								

OSPREY

	SEASON	OCEAN	SHORE	SALT	FRESH	GRASS	DESERT	SCRUB	O WOODS	D WOODS	C WOODS	FARMS	TOWNS
Osprey	R		X	X	X								

	SEASON	OCEAN	SHORE	SALT	FRESH	GRASS	DESERT	SCRUB	O WOODS	D WOODS	C WOODS	FARMS	TOWNS

FALCONS

	SEASON	OCEAN	SHORE	SALT	FRESH	GRASS	DESERT	SCRUB	O WOODS	D WOODS	C WOODS	FARMS	TOWNS
Peregrine Falcon	W		X		X	X							
Merlin	W		X		X				X		X		
American Kestrel	R				X			X	X			X	

GROUSE

	SEASON	OCEAN	SHORE	SALT	FRESH	GRASS	DESERT	SCRUB	O WOODS	D WOODS	C WOODS	FARMS	TOWNS
Ruffed Grouse	R								X	X	X	X	

QUAIL & PHEASANTS

	SEASON	OCEAN	SHORE	SALT	FRESH	GRASS	DESERT	SCRUB	O WOODS	D WOODS	C WOODS	FARMS	TOWNS
Bobwhite	R					X		X				X	
Black Francolin	R					X		X				X	

TURKEYS

	SEASON	OCEAN	SHORE	SALT	FRESH	GRASS	DESERT	SCRUB	O WOODS	D WOODS	C WOODS	FARMS	TOWNS
Wild Turkey	R								X	X	X	X	

CRANES

	SEASON	OCEAN	SHORE	SALT	FRESH	GRASS	DESERT	SCRUB	O WOODS	D WOODS	C WOODS	FARMS	TOWNS
Sandhill Crane	R				X	X						X	

RAILS

	SEASON	OCEAN	SHORE	SALT	FRESH	GRASS	DESERT	SCRUB	O WOODS	D WOODS	C WOODS	FARMS	TOWNS
King Rail	R			X	X								
Clapper Rail	R			X									
Virginia Rail	R			X	X								
Sora	W			X	X							X	
Purple Gallinule	R				X								

	SEASON	OCEAN	SHORE	SALT	FRESH	GRASS	DESERT	SCRUB	O WOODS	D WOODS	C WOODS	FARMS	TOWNS
RAILS, *continued*													
Common Gallinule (Moorhen)	R				X								
American Coot	R			X	X							X	
OYSTERCATCHERS													
American Oystercatcher	R		X	X									
STILTS & AVOCETS													
American Avocet	W		X	X	X								
Black-necked Stilt	B		X	X	X								
PLOVERS													
Semipalmated Plover	W		X	X	X								
Killdeer	R		X	X	X	X						X	
Piping Plover	W		X	X	X								
Snowy Plover	R		X	X	X								
Lesser Golden Plover	M		X	X	X	X						X	
Black-bellied Plover	W		X	X	X	X						X	
GODWITS													
Marbled Godwit	W		X	X	X	X							
CURLEWS													
Whimbrel	W		X	X	X	X							

	SEASON	OCEAN	SHORE	SALT	FRESH	GRASS	DESERT	SCRUB	O WOODS	D WOODS	C WOODS	FARMS	TOWNS
UPLAND SANDPIPERS													
Upland Sandpiper	M					X						X	
Solitary Sandpiper	M				X								
Spotted Sandpiper	R		X	X	X	X							
Willet	R		X	X	X								
Greater Yellowlegs	W				X	X							
Lesser Yellowlegs	W			X	X	X							
WOODCOCK													
American Woodcock	R							X	X	X		X	
SNIPE													
Common Snipe	W			X	X	X							
SANDPIPERS													
Short-billed Dowitcher	W		X	X	X								
Long-billed Dowitcher	W		X	X	X								
Red Knot	W		X	X	X								
Sanderling	W		X	X	X								
Semipalmated Sandpiper	M		X	X	X								
Western Sandpiper	W		X	X	X								
Least Sandpiper	W		X	X	X								
Pectoral Sandpiper	M			X	X								
Ruddy Turnstone	W		X	X									
Dunlin	W	X											

	SEASON	OCEAN	SHORE	SALT	FRESH	GRASS	DESERT	SCRUB	O WOODS	D WOODS	C WOODS	FARMS	TOWNS
GULLS													
Great Black-backed Gull	R	X	X	X									X
Herring Gull	R	X	X	X	X							X	X
Ring-billed Gull	W	X	X	X								X	X
Laughing Gull	R	X	X									X	X
Bonaparte's Gull	W	X	X	X									X
TERNS													
Forster's Tern	R			X	X								
Royal Tern	R	X	X										
Caspian Tern	R	X	X	X									
Black Tern	M	X	X	X								X	
SKIMMERS													
Black Skimmer	R		X	X									
PIGEONS & DOVES													
Rock Dove	R											X	X
Mourning Dove	R					X		X				X	X
Ground Dove	R					X		X				X	
CUCKOOS													
Yellow-billed Cuckoo	B							X	X	X		X	
Black-billed Cuckoo	B							X	X			X	

	SEASON	OCEAN	SHORE	SALT	FRESH	GRASS	DESERT	SCRUB	O WOODS	D WOODS	C WOODS	FARMS	TOWNS

OWLS

	SEASON	OCEAN	SHORE	SALT	FRESH	GRASS	DESERT	SCRUB	O WOODS	D WOODS	C WOODS	FARMS	TOWNS
Barn Owl	R				X			X	X			X	X
Eastern Screech Owl	R								X	X		X	X
Great Horned Owl	R				X			X	X	X	X	X	X
Barred Owl	R				X				X	X			
Long-eared Owl	R							X	X	X	X		
Short-eared Owl	W		X	X		X						X	
Saw-whet Owl	R								X	X			

GOATSUCKERS

	SEASON	OCEAN	SHORE	SALT	FRESH	GRASS	DESERT	SCRUB	O WOODS	D WOODS	C WOODS	FARMS	TOWNS
Chuck-will's-widow	R							X	X	X	X		
Whip-poor-will	R							X	X	X	X		
Common Nighthawk	B					X			X			X	X

SWIFTS

	SEASON	OCEAN	SHORE	SALT	FRESH	GRASS	DESERT	SCRUB	O WOODS	D WOODS	C WOODS	FARMS	TOWNS
Chimney Swift	B								X			X	X

HUMMINGBIRDS

	SEASON	OCEAN	SHORE	SALT	FRESH	GRASS	DESERT	SCRUB	O WOODS	D WOODS	C WOODS	FARMS	TOWNS
Ruby-throated Hummingbird	B							X	X	X	X	X	

KINGFISHERS

	SEASON	OCEAN	SHORE	SALT	FRESH	GRASS	DESERT	SCRUB	O WOODS	D WOODS	C WOODS	FARMS	TOWNS
Belted Kingfisher	R		X	X	X								

	SEASON	OCEAN	SHORE	SALT	FRESH	GRASS	DESERT	SCRUB	O WOODS	D WOODS	C WOODS	FARMS	TOWNS
WOODPECKERS													
Common Flicker	R							X	X	X	X	X	X
Pileated Woodpecker	R								X	X			
Red-bellied Woodpecker	R							X	X	X	X	X	X
Red-headed Woodpecker	R					X		X	X			X	X
Yellow-bellied Sapsucker	W								X	X		X	X
Hairy Woodpecker	R								X	X	X	X	X
Downy Woodpecker	R								X	X	X	X	X
FLYCATCHERS													
Eastern Kingbird	B				X			X	X			X	X
Great Crested Flycatcher	B							X	X	X		X	X
Eastern Phoebe	R							X	X	X		X	X
Yellow-bellied Flycatcher	M							X	X		X		
Acadian Flycatcher	B								X	X			
Alder Flycatcher	M							X	X	X			
Willow Flycatcher	M							X	X	X			
Least Flycatcher	B							X	X	X		X	X
Eastern Wood Pewee	B								X	X	X	X	X
Olive-sided Flycatcher	M								X		X		
LARKS													
Horned Lark	R		X			X						X	X
SWALLOWS													
Tree Swallow	R		X	X	X	X						X	X

SWALLOWS, *continued*

	SEASON	OCEAN	SHORE	SALT	FRESH	GRASS	DESERT	SCRUB	O WOODS	D WOODS	C WOODS	FARMS	TOWNS
Bank Swallow	B				X	X						X	X
Rough-winged Swallow	R				X							X	X
Cliff Swallow	B				X	X						X	X
Barn Swallow	B				X	X						X	X
Purple Martin	B									X		X	X

JAYS & CROWS

	SEASON	OCEAN	SHORE	SALT	FRESH	GRASS	DESERT	SCRUB	O WOODS	D WOODS	C WOODS	FARMS	TOWNS
Blue Jay	R								X	X	X	X	X
Common Raven	R		X			X	X	X	X	X	X	X	
Common Crow	R					X			X	X	X	X	X
Fish Crow	R	X	X	X									

TITMICE

	SEASON	OCEAN	SHORE	SALT	FRESH	GRASS	DESERT	SCRUB	O WOODS	D WOODS	C WOODS	FARMS	TOWNS
Black-capped Chickadee	R								X	X	X	X	X
Carolina Chickadee	R								X	X		X	X
Tufted Titmouse	R								X	X		X	X

NUTHATCHES

	SEASON	OCEAN	SHORE	SALT	FRESH	GRASS	DESERT	SCRUB	O WOODS	D WOODS	C WOODS	FARMS	TOWNS
White-breasted Nuthatch	B								X	X	X	X	X
Red-breasted Nuthatch	W								X	X	X		
Brown-headed Nuthatch	R								X	X	X		

CREEPERS

	SEASON	OCEAN	SHORE	SALT	FRESH	GRASS	DESERT	SCRUB	O WOODS	D WOODS	C WOODS	FARMS	TOWNS
Brown Creeper	R								X	X			

	SEASON	OCEAN	SHORE	SALT	FRESH	GRASS	DESERT	SCRUB	O WOODS	D WOODS	C WOODS	FARMS	TOWNS

WRENS

	SEASON	OCEAN	SHORE	SALT	FRESH	GRASS	DESERT	SCRUB	O WOODS	D WOODS	C WOODS	FARMS	TOWNS
House Wren	R							X	X			X	X
Winter Wren	R							X		X	X		
Carolina Wren	R							X	X			X	X
Marsh Wren	R				X			X					
Sedge Wren	W			X	X								

THRASHERS

	SEASON	OCEAN	SHORE	SALT	FRESH	GRASS	DESERT	SCRUB	O WOODS	D WOODS	C WOODS	FARMS	TOWNS
Mockingbird	R							X	X	X		X	X
Catbird	R							X	X	X		X	X
Brown Thrasher	R							X	X			X	X

THRUSHES

	SEASON	OCEAN	SHORE	SALT	FRESH	GRASS	DESERT	SCRUB	O WOODS	D WOODS	C WOODS	FARMS	TOWNS
American Robin	R							X	X			X	X
Wood Thrush	B								X	X			X
Hermit Thrush	W								X	X	X		
Swainson's Thrush	M								X	X	X		
Gray-cheeked Thrush	M								X	X	X		
Veery	B								X	X			
Eastern Bluebird	R						X		X			X	X
Blue-gray Gnatcatcher	R								X	X	X		
Golden-crowned Kinglet	R										X		
Ruby-crowned Kinglet	W								X	X	X	X	

PIPITS

	SEASON	OCEAN	SHORE	SALT	FRESH	GRASS	DESERT	SCRUB	O WOODS	D WOODS	C WOODS	FARMS	TOWNS
Water Pipit	W		X			X						X	X

WAXWINGS

	SEASON	OCEAN	SHORE	SALT	FRESH	GRASS	DESERT	SCRUB	O WOODS	D WOODS	C WOODS	FARMS	TOWNS
Cedar Waxwing	R							X	X	X	X	X	X

	SEASON	OCEAN	SHORE	SALT	FRESH	GRASS	DESERT	SCRUB	O WOODS	D WOODS	C WOODS	FARMS	TOWNS

SHRIKES

	SEASON	OCEAN	SHORE	SALT	FRESH	GRASS	DESERT	SCRUB	O WOODS	D WOODS	C WOODS	FARMS	TOWNS
Loggerhead Shrike	R					X	X	X	X			X	

STARLINGS

	SEASON	OCEAN	SHORE	SALT	FRESH	GRASS	DESERT	SCRUB	O WOODS	D WOODS	C WOODS	FARMS	TOWNS
Starling	R											X	X

VIREOS

	SEASON	OCEAN	SHORE	SALT	FRESH	GRASS	DESERT	SCRUB	O WOODS	D WOODS	C WOODS	FARMS	TOWNS
Solitary Vireo	R								X	X			
White-eyed Vireo	R							X				X	
Yellow-throated Vireo	R								X	X		X	X
Red-eyed Vireo	B								X	X		X	X
Warbling Vireo	B								X	X		X	X

WARBLERS

	SEASON	OCEAN	SHORE	SALT	FRESH	GRASS	DESERT	SCRUB	O WOODS	D WOODS	C WOODS	FARMS	TOWNS
Black-and-white Warbler	R								X	X			
Prothonotary Warbler	B				X				X	X			
Blue-winged Warbler	B							X	X			X	
Tennessee Warbler	M							X	X	X	X		
Orange-crowned Warbler	W							X	X	X			
Nashville Warbler	M							X	X	X	X		
Northern Parula	B							X	X	X	X	X	
Yellow Warbler	B				X			X	X			X	
Magnolia Warbler	B							X	X	X	X		
Yellow-rumped Warbler	W							X	X	X	X		
Black-throated Green Warbler	B								X	X	X		
Black-throated Blue Warbler	B							X	X	X	X		

WARBLERS, continued

	SEASON	OCEAN	SHORE	SALT	FRESH	GRASS	DESERT	SCRUB	O WOODS	D WOODS	C WOODS	FARMS	TOWNS
Cerulean Warbler	B								X	X			
Yellow-throated Warbler	R								X	X	X		
Blackburnian Warbler	B								X	X	X		
Chestnut-sided Warbler	B							X	X	X		X	
Bay-breasted Warbler	M								X	X	X		
Blackpoll Warbler	M								X	X	X		
Pine Warbler	R										X		
Prairie Warbler	B							X	X	X	X		
Palm Warbler	W							X				X	
Ovenbird	R								X	X	X		
Northern Waterthrush	M				X				X	X	X		
Louisiana Waterthrush	B				X					X			
Common Yellowthroat	R							X	X			X	
Yellow-breasted Chat	B							X	X				
Kentucky Warbler	B									X			
Hooded Warbler	B									X			
Wilson's Warbler	M							X	X	X			
Canada Warbler	B							X	X	X	X		
American Redstart	B							X	X	X			

WEAVER FINCHES

	SEASON	OCEAN	SHORE	SALT	FRESH	GRASS	DESERT	SCRUB	O WOODS	D WOODS	C WOODS	FARMS	TOWNS
House Sparrow	R											X	X

BLACKBIRDS

	SEASON	OCEAN	SHORE	SALT	FRESH	GRASS	DESERT	SCRUB	O WOODS	D WOODS	C WOODS	FARMS	TOWNS
Bobolink	B				X	X						X	
Eastern Meadowlark	R					X						X	
Western Meadowlark	W					X						X	
Red-winged Blackbird	R			X	X	X						X	

BLACKBIRDS, *continued*

	SEASON	OCEAN	SHORE	SALT	FRESH	GRASS	DESERT	SCRUB	O WOODS	D WOODS	C WOODS	FARMS	TOWNS
Orchard Oriole	B								X			X	X
Northern Oriole	B								X	X		X	X
Rusty Blackbird	W				X				X	X	X		
Brewer's Blackbird	W					X						X	X
Boat-tailed Grackle	R		X	X								X	
Common Grackle	R								X			X	X
Brown-headed Cowbird	R								X			X	X

TANAGERS

	SEASON	OCEAN	SHORE	SALT	FRESH	GRASS	DESERT	SCRUB	O WOODS	D WOODS	C WOODS	FARMS	TOWNS
Scarlet Tanager	B								X	X			
Summer Tanager	B								X	X	X		

CARDINALS & BUNTINGS

	SEASON	OCEAN	SHORE	SALT	FRESH	GRASS	DESERT	SCRUB	O WOODS	D WOODS	C WOODS	FARMS	TOWNS
Cardinal	R								X	X		X	X
Rose-breasted Grosbeak	B								X	X	X	X	X
Blue Grosbeak	B								X			X	
Indigo Bunting	B								X	X		X	
Painted Bunting	B								X	X			
Dickcissel	B					X						X	

FINCHES

	SEASON	OCEAN	SHORE	SALT	FRESH	GRASS	DESERT	SCRUB	O WOODS	D WOODS	C WOODS	FARMS	TOWNS
Evening Grosbeak	W								X	X	X	X	X
Purple Finch	W									X	X	X	X
House Finch	R					X	X	X				X	X
Pine Siskin	W									X	X		
American Goldfinch	R				X		X					X	X

SPARROWS

	SEASON	OCEAN	SHORE	SALT	FRESH	GRASS	DESERT	SCRUB	O WOODS	D WOODS	C WOODS	FARMS	TOWNS
Rufous-sided Towhee	R							X	X			X	X
Savannah Sparrow	R		X	X		X						X	
Grasshopper Sparrow	R					X						X	
Le Conte's Sparrow	W				X	X						X	
Sharp-tailed Sparrow	R			X	X								
Seaside Sparrow	R			X				X					
Vesper Sparrow	R					X						X	
Lark Sparrow	R					X		X	X			X	
Dark-eyed Junco	R								X	X	X	X	X
Chipping Sparrow	R					X		X	X			X	X
Field Sparrow	R					X		X				X	
White-crowned Sparrow	W					X		X	X			X	X
White-throated Sparrow	R							X		X	X	X	X
Fox Sparrow	W							X		X	X	X	
Lincoln's Sparrow	W					X		X	X	X			
Swamp Sparrow	R				X			X	X			X	
Song Sparrow	R		X	X	X			X	X	X		X	X

CHECKLIST OF FLORIDA BIRDS

	SEASON	OCEAN	SHORE	SALT	FRESH	GRASS	DESERT	SCRUB	O WOODS	D WOODS	C WOODS	FARMS	TOWNS
LOONS													
Common Loon	W	X	X	X	X								
GREBES													
Horned Grebe	W		X	X	X								
Pied-billed Grebe	R		X	X	X								
PELICANS													
Brown Pelican	R	X	X	X									
White Pelican	W		X	X	X								
FRIGATEBIRDS													
Magnificent Frigatebird	M		X	X									
BOOBIES & GANNETS													
Northern Gannet	W	X	X										
CORMORANTS													
Double-crested Cormorant	R		X	X	X								

	SEASON	OCEAN	SHORE	SALT	FRESH	GRASS	DESERT	SCRUB	O WOODS	D WOODS	C WOODS	FARMS	TOWNS

ANHINGAS

	SEASON	OCEAN	SHORE	SALT	FRESH	GRASS	DESERT	SCRUB	O WOODS	D WOODS	C WOODS	FARMS	TOWNS
Anhinga	R			X	X								

HERONS & BITTERNS

	SEASON	OCEAN	SHORE	SALT	FRESH	GRASS	DESERT	SCRUB	O WOODS	D WOODS	C WOODS	FARMS	TOWNS
Great Blue Heron	R			X	X								
Green-backed Heron	R			X	X								
Little Blue Heron	R			X	X								
Cattle Egret	R			X	X	X						X	
Tricolored Heron	R			X									
Great Egret	R			X	X								
Snowy Egret	R			X	X							X	
Black-crowned Night-heron	R			X	X								
Yellow-crowned Night-heron	R			X	X								
American Bittern	R			X	X								
Least Bittern	R				X								

STORKS

	SEASON	OCEAN	SHORE	SALT	FRESH	GRASS	DESERT	SCRUB	O WOODS	D WOODS	C WOODS	FARMS	TOWNS
Wood Stork	R		X	X	X								

IBISES

	SEASON	OCEAN	SHORE	SALT	FRESH	GRASS	DESERT	SCRUB	O WOODS	D WOODS	C WOODS	FARMS	TOWNS
Glossy Ibis	R			X	X								
White Ibis	R			X	X								
Roseate Spoonbill	R			X									

FLAMINGOS

	SEASON	OCEAN	SHORE	SALT	FRESH	GRASS	DESERT	SCRUB	O WOODS	D WOODS	C WOODS	FARMS	TOWNS
American Flamingo	M			X									

	SEASON	OCEAN	SHORE	SALT	FRESH	GRASS	DESERT	SCRUB	O WOODS	D WOODS	C WOODS	FARMS	TOWNS

MARSH DUCKS

	SEASON	OCEAN	SHORE	SALT	FRESH	GRASS	DESERT	SCRUB	O WOODS	D WOODS	C WOODS	FARMS	TOWNS
Mottled Duck	R		X	X	X								
Pintail	W			X	X								
American Wigeon	W			X	X	X							
Northern Shoveler	W			X	X								
Blue-winged Teal	W			X	X								
Green-winged Teal	W			X	X								
Wood Duck	R				X								

WHISTLING DUCKS

	SEASON	OCEAN	SHORE	SALT	FRESH	GRASS	DESERT	SCRUB	O WOODS	D WOODS	C WOODS	FARMS	TOWNS
Fulvous Whistling Duck	R				X	X						X	

DIVING DUCKS

	SEASON	OCEAN	SHORE	SALT	FRESH	GRASS	DESERT	SCRUB	O WOODS	D WOODS	C WOODS	FARMS	TOWNS
Redhead	W			X	X								
Canvasback	W			X	X								
Ring-necked Duck	W			X	X								
Lesser Scaup	W		X	X	X								
Common Goldeneye	W		X	X	X								
Bufflehead	W		X	X	X								

STIFF-TAILED DUCKS

	SEASON	OCEAN	SHORE	SALT	FRESH	GRASS	DESERT	SCRUB	O WOODS	D WOODS	C WOODS	FARMS	TOWNS
Ruddy Duck	W		X	X	X								

MERGANSERS

	SEASON	OCEAN	SHORE	SALT	FRESH	GRASS	DESERT	SCRUB	O WOODS	D WOODS	C WOODS	FARMS	TOWNS
Red-breasted Merganser	W		X	X	X								
Hooded Merganser	W			X	X								

	SEASON	OCEAN	SHORE	SALT	FRESH	GRASS	DESERT	SCRUB	O WOODS	D WOODS	C WOODS	FARMS	TOWNS
VULTURES													
Turkey Vulture	R					X			X			X	
Black Vulture	R					X			X			X	
KITES													
Mississippi Kite	B							X	X	X			
Swallow-tailed Kite	B				X			X	X				
Snail Kite	R				X								
ACCIPITERS													
Sharp-shinned Hawk	W								X	X	X		
HARRIERS													
Northern Harrier	W				X	X							
BUTEOS													
Red-tailed Hawk	W				X			X	X	X		X	
Red-shouldered Hawk	R				X				X	X		X	
Broad-winged Hawk	M								X	X			
EAGLES													
Bald Eagle	R		X	X	X								

	SEASON	OCEAN	SHORE	SALT	FRESH	GRASS	DESERT	SCRUB	O WOODS	D WOODS	C WOODS	FARMS	TOWNS

OSPREY

Osprey — R, X SHORE, X SALT, X FRESH

CARACARAS

Caracara — R, X GRASS, X DESERT, X FARMS

FALCONS

Peregrine Falcon — W, X OCEAN, X SALT, X FRESH

American Kestrel — R, X FRESH, X DESERT, X SCRUB, X FARMS

QUAIL & PHEASANTS

Bobwhite — R, X GRASS, X SCRUB, X O WOODS, X FARMS

TURKEYS

Wild Turkey — R, X O WOODS, X D WOODS, X C WOODS, X FARMS

CRANES

Sandhill Crane — R, X FRESH, X GRASS, X FARMS

	SEASON	OCEAN	SHORE	SALT	FRESH	GRASS	DESERT	SCRUB	O WOODS	D WOODS	C WOODS	FARMS	TOWNS

LIMPKINS
Limpkin	R				X								

RAILS
King Rail	R		X	X									
Clapper Rail	R			X									
Virginia Rail	W			X	X								
Sora	W			X	X								X
Purple Gallinule	R				X								
Common Gallinule (Moorhen)	R				X								
American Coot	R			X	X								X

OYSTERCATCHERS
American Oystercatcher	R		X	X									

STILTS & AVOCETS
American Avocet	W		X	X	X								
Black-necked Stilt	W		X	X	X	X							

PLOVERS
Semipalmated Plover	W		X	X	X								
Killdeer	R		X	X	X	X							X
Piping Plover	W		X	X	X								
Black-bellied Plover	W		X	X	X	X							X

	SEASON	OCEAN	SHORE	SALT	FRESH	GRASS	DESERT	SCRUB	O WOODS	D WOODS	C WOODS	FARMS	TOWNS

GODWITS

	SEASON	OCEAN	SHORE	SALT	FRESH	GRASS	DESERT	SCRUB	O WOODS	D WOODS	C WOODS	FARMS	TOWNS
Marbled Godwit	W		X	X	X	X							

CURLEWS

	SEASON	OCEAN	SHORE	SALT	FRESH	GRASS	DESERT	SCRUB	O WOODS	D WOODS	C WOODS	FARMS	TOWNS
Whimbrel	M		X	X	X	X							

UPLAND SANDPIPERS

	SEASON	OCEAN	SHORE	SALT	FRESH	GRASS	DESERT	SCRUB	O WOODS	D WOODS	C WOODS	FARMS	TOWNS
Spotted Sandpiper	W		X	X	X	X							
Willet	R		X	X	X								
Greater Yellowlegs	W				X	X							
Lesser Yellowlegs	W			X	X	X							

WOODCOCK

	SEASON	OCEAN	SHORE	SALT	FRESH	GRASS	DESERT	SCRUB	O WOODS	D WOODS	C WOODS	FARMS	TOWNS
American Woodcock	R								X	X	X		X

SNIPE

	SEASON	OCEAN	SHORE	SALT	FRESH	GRASS	DESERT	SCRUB	O WOODS	D WOODS	C WOODS	FARMS	TOWNS
Common Snipe	W				X	X	X						

SANDPIPERS

	SEASON	OCEAN	SHORE	SALT	FRESH	GRASS	DESERT	SCRUB	O WOODS	D WOODS	C WOODS	FARMS	TOWNS
Short-billed Dowitcher	W		X	X	X								
Red Knot	M		X	X	X								
Sanderling	W		X	X	X								
Semipalmated Sandpiper	M		X	X	X								

SANDPIPERS, *continued*

	SEASON	OCEAN	SHORE	SALT	FRESH	GRASS	DESERT	SCRUB	O WOODS	D WOODS	C WOODS	FARMS	TOWNS
Western Sandpiper	W		X	X	X								
Least Sandpiper	W		X	X	X								
Ruddy Turnstone	W		X	X									
Dunlin	W		X										

GULLS

	SEASON	OCEAN	SHORE	SALT	FRESH	GRASS	DESERT	SCRUB	O WOODS	D WOODS	C WOODS	FARMS	TOWNS
Herring Gull	W		X	X	X	X						X	X
Ring-billed Gull	W		X	X	X							X	X
Laughing Gull	R		X	X								X	X
Bonaparte's Gull	W		X	X	X								X

TERNS

	SEASON	OCEAN	SHORE	SALT	FRESH	GRASS	DESERT	SCRUB	O WOODS	D WOODS	C WOODS	FARMS	TOWNS
Forster's Tern	R			X	X								
Least Tern	B		X	X	X							X	X
Royal Tern	R		X	X									
Black Tern	M		X	X	X							X	

SKIMMERS

	SEASON	OCEAN	SHORE	SALT	FRESH	GRASS	DESERT	SCRUB	O WOODS	D WOODS	C WOODS	FARMS	TOWNS
Black Skimmer	R		X	X									

PIGEONS & DOVES

	SEASON	OCEAN	SHORE	SALT	FRESH	GRASS	DESERT	SCRUB	O WOODS	D WOODS	C WOODS	FARMS	TOWNS
White-crowned Pigeon	B				X				X	X			

PIGEONS & DOVES, *continued*

	SEASON	OCEAN	SHORE	SALT	FRESH	GRASS	DESERT	SCRUB	O WOODS	D WOODS	C WOODS	FARMS	TOWNS
Rock Dove	R											X	X
Mourning Dove	R					X		X				X	X
Ringed Turtle Dove	R												X
Ground Dove	R					X		X				X	

PARROTS

	SEASON	OCEAN	SHORE	SALT	FRESH	GRASS	DESERT	SCRUB	O WOODS	D WOODS	C WOODS	FARMS	TOWNS
Budgerigar	R					X		X				X	X
Canary-winged Parakeet	R					X		X				X	

CUCKOOS

	SEASON	OCEAN	SHORE	SALT	FRESH	GRASS	DESERT	SCRUB	O WOODS	D WOODS	C WOODS	FARMS	TOWNS
Mangrove Cuckoo	R		X	X									
Yellow-billed Cuckoo	B							X	X	X		X	
Smooth-billed Ani	R					X		X				X	

OWLS

	SEASON	OCEAN	SHORE	SALT	FRESH	GRASS	DESERT	SCRUB	O WOODS	D WOODS	C WOODS	FARMS	TOWNS
Barn Owl	R					X		X	X			X	X
Eastern Screech Owl	R								X	X		X	X
Great Horned Owl	R					X		X	X	X	X	X	X
Barred Owl	R				X				X	X			

GOATSUCKERS

	SEASON	OCEAN	SHORE	SALT	FRESH	GRASS	DESERT	SCRUB	O WOODS	D WOODS	C WOODS	FARMS	TOWNS
Chuck-will's-widow	R							X	X	X	X		
Whip-poor-will	W							X	X	X	X		
Common Nighthawk	B					X		X				X	X

SWIFTS

	SEASON	OCEAN	SHORE	SALT	FRESH	GRASS	DESERT	SCRUB	O WOODS	D WOODS	C WOODS	FARMS	TOWNS
Chimney Swift	B										X	X	X

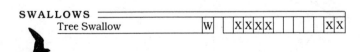

	SEASON	OCEAN	SHORE	SALT	FRESH	GRASS	DESERT	SCRUB	O WOODS	D WOODS	C WOODS	FARMS	TOWNS
HUMMINGBIRDS													
Ruby-throated Hummingbird	B								X	X	X	X	X
KINGFISHERS													
Belted Kingfisher	R	X	X	X									
WOODPECKERS													
Common Flicker	R							X	X	X	X	X	X
Pileated Woodpecker	R								X	X			
Red-bellied Woodpecker	R							X	X	X	X	X	X
Yellow-bellied Sapsucker	W								X	X	X	X	X
Downy Woodpecker	R								X	X	X	X	X
FLYCATCHERS													
Eastern Kingbird	B				X			X	X			X	X
Gray Kingbird	B							X	X	X		X	
Great Crested Flycatcher	B							X	X	X		X	
Eastern Phoebe	W							X	X	X		X	X
Acadian Flycatcher	B								X	X			
Eastern Wood Pewee	B							X	X	X	X	X	
SWALLOWS													
Tree Swallow	W		X	X	X	X						X	X

SWALLOWS, *continued*

	SEASON	OCEAN	SHORE	SALT	FRESH	GRASS	DESERT	SCRUB	O WOODS	D WOODS	C WOODS	FARMS	TOWNS
Bank Swallow	M				X	X						X	X
Rough-winged Swallow	M				X							X	X
Barn Swallow	B				X	X						X	X
Purple Martin	B								X			X	X

JAYS & CROWS

	SEASON	OCEAN	SHORE	SALT	FRESH	GRASS	DESERT	SCRUB	O WOODS	D WOODS	C WOODS	FARMS	TOWNS
Blue Jay	R								X	X	X	X	X
Scrub Jay	R						X	X	X				X
Common Crow	R						X	X	X	X		X	X
Fish Crow	R		X	X	X								

TITMICE

	SEASON	OCEAN	SHORE	SALT	FRESH	GRASS	DESERT	SCRUB	O WOODS	D WOODS	C WOODS	FARMS	TOWNS
Carolina Chickadee	R								X	X		X	X
Tufted Titmouse	R								X	X		X	X

NUTHATCHES

	SEASON	OCEAN	SHORE	SALT	FRESH	GRASS	DESERT	SCRUB	O WOODS	D WOODS	C WOODS	FARMS	TOWNS
Brown-headed Nuthatch	R								X	X	X		

BULBUL

	SEASON	OCEAN	SHORE	SALT	FRESH	GRASS	DESERT	SCRUB	O WOODS	D WOODS	C WOODS	FARMS	TOWNS
Red-whiskered Bulbul	R								X	X		X	X

WRENS

	SEASON	OCEAN	SHORE	SALT	FRESH	GRASS	DESERT	SCRUB	O WOODS	D WOODS	C WOODS	FARMS	TOWNS
House Wren	W							X	X			X	X
Carolina Wren	R							X	X			X	X

	SEASON	OCEAN	SHORE	SALT	FRESH	GRASS	DESERT	SCRUB	O WOODS	D WOODS	C WOODS	FARMS	TOWNS
THRASHERS													
Mockingbird	R							X	X	X		X	X
Catbird	W							X	X	X		X	X
Brown Thrasher	W							X	X			X	X
THRUSHES													
American Robin	R							X	X			X	X
Wood Thrush	M								X	X			X
Hermit Thrush	W								X	X	X		
Eastern Bluebird	R					X			X			X	X
Blue-gray Gnatcatcher	R								X	X	X		
Ruby-crowned Kinglet	W								X	X	X	X	
PIPITS													
Water Pipit	W		X		X							X	X
SHRIKES													
Loggerhead Shrike	R					X	X	X	X			X	
STARLINGS													
Starling	R											X	X
VIREOS													
Solitary Vireo	W									X	X		
White-eyed Vireo	R							X				X	
Yellow-throated Vireo	R								X	X		X	X
Black-whiskered Vireo	B			X	X			X				X	X
Red-eyed Vireo	B								X	X		X	X

WARBLERS

	SEASON	OCEAN	SHORE	SALT	FRESH	GRASS	DESERT	SCRUB	O WOODS	D WOODS	C WOODS	FARMS	TOWNS
Black-and-white Warbler	W								X	X			
Prothonotary Warbler	B				X				X	X			
Orange-crowned Warbler	W							X	X	X			
Northern Parula	R							X	X	X	X	X	
Magnolia Warbler	M							X	X	X	X		
Cape May Warbler	M								X	X	X		
Yellow-rumped Warbler	W							X	X	X	X		
Black-throated Blue Warbler	M							X	X	X	X		
Yellow-throated Warbler	R								X	X	X		
Blackburnian Warbler	M								X	X	X		
Chestnut-sided Warbler	M							X	X	X		X	
Blackpoll Warbler	M								X	X	X		
Pine Warbler	R								X		X		
Prairie Warbler	R							X	X	X	X		
Palm Warbler	W							X				X	
Ovenbird	W								X	X	X		
Northern Waterthrush	M				X				X	X	X		
Louisiana Waterthrush	M				X					X			
Common Yellowthroat	R							X	X			X	
Yellow-breasted Chat	B							X	X				
Kentucky Warbler	B									X			
Hooded Warbler	B									X			
American Redstart	M								X	X	X		

WEAVER FINCHES

	SEASON	OCEAN	SHORE	SALT	FRESH	GRASS	DESERT	SCRUB	O WOODS	D WOODS	C WOODS	FARMS	TOWNS
House Sparrow	R											X	X

BLACKBIRDS

	SEASON	OCEAN	SHORE	SALT	FRESH	GRASS	DESERT	SCRUB	O WOODS	D WOODS	C WOODS	FARMS	TOWNS
Eastern Meadowlark	R					X						X	

BLACKBIRDS, *continued*

	SEASON	OCEAN	SHORE	SALT	FRESH	GRASS	DESERT	SCRUB	O WOODS	D WOODS	C WOODS	FARMS	TOWNS
Red-winged Blackbird	R			X	X	X						X	
Orchard Oriole	B							X				X	X
Spotted-breasted Oriole	R							X				X	X
Rusty Blackbird	W				X			X	X	X			
Brewer's Blackbird	W					X						X	X
Boat-tailed Grackle	R		X	X								X	
Common Grackle	R							X				X	X
Brown-headed Cowbird	R							X				X	X

TANAGERS

	SEASON	OCEAN	SHORE	SALT	FRESH	GRASS	DESERT	SCRUB	O WOODS	D WOODS	C WOODS	FARMS	TOWNS
Scarlet Tanager	M								X	X			
Summer Tanager	B							X	X	X			

CARDINALS

	SEASON	OCEAN	SHORE	SALT	FRESH	GRASS	DESERT	SCRUB	O WOODS	D WOODS	C WOODS	FARMS	TOWNS
Cardinal	R							X	X			X	X
Rose-breasted Grosbeak	M							X	X	X		X	X
Blue Grosbeak	B							X				X	
Indigo Bunting	R							X	X			X	
Painted Bunting	R							X	X				

FINCHES

	SEASON	OCEAN	SHORE	SALT	FRESH	GRASS	DESERT	SCRUB	O WOODS	D WOODS	C WOODS	FARMS	TOWNS
Purple Finch	W								X	X	X	X	
Pine Siskin	W								X	X			
American Goldfinch	W					X		X				X	X

SPARROWS

	SEASON	OCEAN	SHORE	SALT	FRESH	GRASS	DESERT	SCRUB	O WOODS	D WOODS	C WOODS	FARMS	TOWNS
Rufous-sided Towhee	R							X	X			X	X
Savannah Sparrow	W		X	X		X						X	

SPARROWS, *continued*

	SEASON	OCEAN	SHORE	SALT	FRESH	GRASS	DESERT	SCRUB	O WOODS	D WOODS	C WOODS	FARMS	TOWNS
Sharp-tailed Sparrow	W			X	X								
Seaside Sparrow	R			X				X					
Vesper Sparrow	W					X						X	
Dark-eyed Junco	W								X	X	X	X	X
Bachman's Sparrow	R							X	X			X	
Chipping Sparrow	W						X	X	X			X	X
Field Sparrow	W						X	X				X	
White-throated Sparrow	W							X	X	X	X	X	X
Fox Sparrow	W							X		X	X	X	
Swamp Sparrow	W				X			X	X			X	X
Song Sparrow	W		X	X	X			X	X	X		X	X

	SEASON	OCEAN	SHORE	SALT	FRESH	GRASS	DESERT	SCRUB	O WOODS	D WOODS	C WOODS	FARMS	TOWNS
LOONS													
Common Loon	M				X								

	SEASON	OCEAN	SHORE	SALT	FRESH	GRASS	DESERT	SCRUB	O WOODS	D WOODS	C WOODS	FARMS	TOWNS
GREBES													
Western Grebe	B				X								
Red-necked Grebe	B				X								
Horned Grebe	B				X								
Eared Grebe	B				X								
Pied-billed Grebe	B				X								

	SEASON	OCEAN	SHORE	SALT	FRESH	GRASS	DESERT	SCRUB	O WOODS	D WOODS	C WOODS	FARMS	TOWNS
PELICANS													
White Pelican	B				X								

	SEASON	OCEAN	SHORE	SALT	FRESH	GRASS	DESERT	SCRUB	O WOODS	D WOODS	C WOODS	FARMS	TOWNS
CORMORANTS													
Double-crested Cormorant	B				X								

	SEASON	OCEAN	SHORE	SALT	FRESH	GRASS	DESERT	SCRUB	O WOODS	D WOODS	C WOODS	FARMS	TOWNS
HERONS & BITTERNS													
Great Blue Heron	R				X								
Green-backed Heron	B				X								
Little Blue Heron	B				X								

HERONS & BITTERNS, *continued*

	SEASON	OCEAN	SHORE	SALT	FRESH	GRASS	DESERT	SCRUB	O WOODS	D WOODS	C WOODS	FARMS	TOWNS
Cattle Egret	B				X	X						X	
Great Egret	B				X								
Black-crowned Night-heron	R				X								
Yellow-crowned Night-heron	B				X								
American Bittern	B				X								
Least Bittern	B				X								

SWANS

	SEASON	OCEAN	SHORE	SALT	FRESH	GRASS	DESERT	SCRUB	O WOODS	D WOODS	C WOODS	FARMS	TOWNS
Tundra Swan	M				X								

GEESE

	SEASON	OCEAN	SHORE	SALT	FRESH	GRASS	DESERT	SCRUB	O WOODS	D WOODS	C WOODS	FARMS	TOWNS
Canada Goose	R				X	X						X	
White-fronted Goose	M				X	X							
Snow Goose	M				X	X							

MARSH DUCKS

	SEASON	OCEAN	SHORE	SALT	FRESH	GRASS	DESERT	SCRUB	O WOODS	D WOODS	C WOODS	FARMS	TOWNS
Mallard	R				X	X							
Black Duck	R				X								
Pintail	R				X								
Gadwall	R				X	X							
American Wigeon	B				X	X							
Northern Shoveler	B				X								
Blue-winged Teal	B				X								
Green-winged Teal	R				X								
Wood Duck	R				X								

	SEASON	OCEAN	SHORE	SALT	FRESH	GRASS	DESERT	SCRUB	O WOODS	D WOODS	C WOODS	FARMS	TOWNS

DIVING DUCKS

	SEASON	OCEAN	SHORE	SALT	FRESH	GRASS	DESERT	SCRUB	O WOODS	D WOODS	C WOODS	FARMS	TOWNS
Redhead	R				X								
Canvasback	W				X								
Ring-necked Duck	B				X								
Greater Scaup	W				X								
Lesser Scaup	R				X								
Common Goldeneye	W				X								
Bufflehead	W				X								
Oldsquaw	W				X								
White-winged Scoter	M				X								
Surf Scoter	M				X								

STIFF-TAILED DUCKS

	SEASON	OCEAN	SHORE	SALT	FRESH	GRASS	DESERT	SCRUB	O WOODS	D WOODS	C WOODS	FARMS	TOWNS
Ruddy Duck	B				X								

MERGANSERS

	SEASON	OCEAN	SHORE	SALT	FRESH	GRASS	DESERT	SCRUB	O WOODS	D WOODS	C WOODS	FARMS	TOWNS
Common Merganser	W				X								
Red-breasted Merganser	W				X								
Hooded Merganser	B				X								

VULTURES

	SEASON	OCEAN	SHORE	SALT	FRESH	GRASS	DESERT	SCRUB	O WOODS	D WOODS	C WOODS	FARMS	TOWNS
Turkey Vulture	R					X	X		X			X	
Black Vulture	R					X	X		X			X	

KITES

	SEASON	OCEAN	SHORE	SALT	FRESH	GRASS	DESERT	SCRUB	O WOODS	D WOODS	C WOODS	FARMS	TOWNS
Mississippi Kite	B								X	X	X		X

	Season	Ocean	Shore	Salt	Fresh	Grass	Desert	Scrub	O Woods	D Woods	C Woods	Farms	Towns
ACCIPITERS													
Goshawk	W								X	X	X	X	
Cooper's Hawk	R								X	X	X	X	
Sharp-shinned Hawk	R									X	X	X	X
HARRIERS													
Northern Harrier	R				X	X						X	
BUTEOS													
Rough-legged Hawk	W				X	X						X	
Red-tailed Hawk	R					X		X	X	X	X	X	X
Red-shouldered Hawk	R								X	X		X	
Swainson's Hawk	B				X	X						X	
Broad-winged Hawk	B								X	X			
EAGLES													
Golden Eagle	M					X		X					
Bald Eagle	W				X	X		X					
OSPREY													
Osprey	B				X								
FALCONS													
Peregrine Falcon	M		X		X	X							
Merlin	M					X		X	X				
American Kestrel	R					X		X	X			X	X

	SEASON	OCEAN	SHORE	SALT	FRESH	GRASS	DESERT	SCRUB	O WOODS	D WOODS	C WOODS	FARMS	TOWNS

GROUSE

	SEASON	OCEAN	SHORE	SALT	FRESH	GRASS	DESERT	SCRUB	O WOODS	D WOODS	C WOODS	FARMS	TOWNS
Spruce Grouse	R										X		
Ruffed Grouse	R								X	X	X		
Sharp-tailed Grouse	R					X		X	X				
Greater Prairie Chicken	R					X							
Lesser Prairie Chicken	R					X							

QUAIL & PHEASANTS

	SEASON	OCEAN	SHORE	SALT	FRESH	GRASS	DESERT	SCRUB	O WOODS	D WOODS	C WOODS	FARMS	TOWNS
Bobwhite	R					X	X					X	
Ring-necked Pheasant	R					X	X					X	
Gray Partridge	R					X						X	

TURKEYS

	SEASON	OCEAN	SHORE	SALT	FRESH	GRASS	DESERT	SCRUB	O WOODS	D WOODS	C WOODS	FARMS	TOWNS
Wild Turkey	R								X	X	X		

CRANES

	SEASON	OCEAN	SHORE	SALT	FRESH	GRASS	DESERT	SCRUB	O WOODS	D WOODS	C WOODS	FARMS	TOWNS
Sandhill Crane	M				X	X						X	
Whooping Crane	M				X	X						X	

RAILS

	SEASON	OCEAN	SHORE	SALT	FRESH	GRASS	DESERT	SCRUB	O WOODS	D WOODS	C WOODS	FARMS	TOWNS
King Rail	B				X								
Virginia Rail	B				X								
Sora	B				X								
Common Gallinule (Moorhen)	B				X								
American Coot	R				X							X	

	SEASON	OCEAN	SHORE	SALT	FRESH	GRASS	DESERT	SCRUB	O WOODS	D WOODS	C WOODS	FARMS	TOWNS

STILTS & AVOCETS

| American Avocet | B | | | | X | | | | | | | | |

PLOVERS

Semipalmated Plover	M		X		X								
Killdeer	R				X	X						X	
Lesser Golden Plover	M		X		X	X						X	
Black-bellied Plover	M		X		X	X						X	

GODWITS

| Hudsonian Godwit | M | | X | | X | | | | | | | | |
| Marbled Godwit | B | | | | X | X | | | | | | | |

CURLEWS

| Whimbrel | M | | X | | X | X | | | | | | | |
| Long-billed Curlew | B | | | | X | X | | | | | | | |

UPLAND SANDPIPERS

Upland Sandpiper	B					X						X	
Solitary Sandpiper	M				X								
Spotted Sandpiper	B				X	X							
Willet	B		X		X								
Greater Yellowlegs	M		X		X								
Lesser Yellowlegs	M		X		X								

WOODCOCK

| American Woodcock | B | | | | | | | X | X | X | | X | |

SNIPE

	SEASON	OCEAN	SHORE	SALT	FRESH	GRASS	DESERT	SCRUB	O WOODS	D WOODS	C WOODS	FARMS	TOWNS
Common Snipe	B				X	X							

SANDPIPERS

	SEASON	OCEAN	SHORE	SALT	FRESH	GRASS	DESERT	SCRUB	O WOODS	D WOODS	C WOODS	FARMS	TOWNS
Short-billed Dowitcher	M		X		X								
Long-billed Dowitcher	M		X		X								
Red Knot	M		X		X								
Sanderling	M		X		X								
Semipalmated Sandpiper	M		X		X								
Western Sandpiper	M		X		X								
Least Sandpiper	M		X		X								
Ruddy Turnstone	M		X		X								
Dunlin	M		X		X								

GULLS

	SEASON	OCEAN	SHORE	SALT	FRESH	GRASS	DESERT	SCRUB	O WOODS	D WOODS	C WOODS	FARMS	TOWNS
Glaucous Gull	W		X		X								X
Great Black-backed Gull	W		X		X								X
Herring Gull	W		X		X	X							X
Ring-billed Gull	R		X		X							X	X
Franklin's Gull	B		X		X	X					X		
Bonaparte's Gull	M		X		X								X

TERNS

	SEASON	OCEAN	SHORE	SALT	FRESH	GRASS	DESERT	SCRUB	O WOODS	D WOODS	C WOODS	FARMS	TOWNS
Forster's Tern	B		X		X								
Common Tern	B		X		X								

TERNS, *continued*

	SEASON	OCEAN	SHORE	SALT	FRESH	GRASS	DESERT	SCRUB	O WOODS	D WOODS	C WOODS	FARMS	TOWNS
Caspian Tern	M		X		X								
Black Tern	B				X							X	

PIGEONS

	SEASON	OCEAN	SHORE	SALT	FRESH	GRASS	DESERT	SCRUB	O WOODS	D WOODS	C WOODS	FARMS	TOWNS
Rock Dove	R											X	X
Mourning Dove	R					X		X				X	X

CUCKOOS

	SEASON	OCEAN	SHORE	SALT	FRESH	GRASS	DESERT	SCRUB	O WOODS	D WOODS	C WOODS	FARMS	TOWNS
Yellow-billed Cuckoo	B							X	X	X		X	
Black-billed Cuckoo	B							X	X			X	

OWLS

	SEASON	OCEAN	SHORE	SALT	FRESH	GRASS	DESERT	SCRUB	O WOODS	D WOODS	C WOODS	FARMS	TOWNS
Barn Owl	R					X		X	X			X	X
Eastern Screech Owl	R								X	X		X	X
Great Horned Owl	R					X		X	X	X	X	X	X
Snowy Owl	W			X	X								
Burrowing Owl	B					X		X				X	X
Barred Owl	R								X	X	X		
Long-eared Owl	R								X	X	X		
Short-eared Owl	R			X	X		X					X	
Saw-whet Owl	R									X	X		

GOATSUCKERS

	SEASON	OCEAN	SHORE	SALT	FRESH	GRASS	DESERT	SCRUB	O WOODS	D WOODS	C WOODS	FARMS	TOWNS
Chuck-will's-widow	B							X	X	X	X		
Whip-poor-will	B							X	X	X	X		
Poor-will	B				X		X	X					
Common Nighthawk	B				X			X				X	X

	SEASON	OCEAN	SHORE	SALT	FRESH	GRASS	DESERT	SCRUB	O WOODS	D WOODS	C WOODS	FARMS	TOWNS

SWIFTS

	SEASON	OCEAN	SHORE	SALT	FRESH	GRASS	DESERT	SCRUB	O WOODS	D WOODS	C WOODS	FARMS	TOWNS
Chimney Swift	B								X			X	X

HUMMINGBIRDS

	SEASON	OCEAN	SHORE	SALT	FRESH	GRASS	DESERT	SCRUB	O WOODS	D WOODS	C WOODS	FARMS	TOWNS
Ruby-throated Hummingbird	B								X	X	X	X	X

KINGFISHERS

	SEASON	OCEAN	SHORE	SALT	FRESH	GRASS	DESERT	SCRUB	O WOODS	D WOODS	C WOODS	FARMS	TOWNS
Belted Kingfisher	R				X								

WOODPECKERS

	SEASON	OCEAN	SHORE	SALT	FRESH	GRASS	DESERT	SCRUB	O WOODS	D WOODS	C WOODS	FARMS	TOWNS
Common Flicker	R							X	X	X	X	X	X
Pileated Woodpecker	R									X	X		
Red-bellied Woodpecker	R								X	X		X	X
Red-headed Woodpecker	R				X			X	X			X	X
Yellow-bellied Sapsucker	M								X	X	X	X	X
Hairy Woodpecker	R								X	X	X	X	X
Downy Woodpecker	R								X	X		X	X
Three-toed Woodpecker	R										X		
Black-backed Woodpecker	W								X		X		

FLYCATCHERS

	SEASON	OCEAN	SHORE	SALT	FRESH	GRASS	DESERT	SCRUB	O WOODS	D WOODS	C WOODS	FARMS	TOWNS
Eastern Kingbird	B					X		X	X			X	X
Western Kingbird	B					X		X	X			X	X
Scissor-tailed Flycatcher	B					X		X	X			X	
Great Crested Flycatcher	B								X	X			
Eastern Phoebe	B								X	X	X		X	X

	SEASON	OCEAN	SHORE	SALT	FRESH	GRASS	DESERT	SCRUB	O WOODS	D WOODS	C WOODS	FARMS	TOWNS

FLYCATCHERS, continued

	SEASON	OCEAN	SHORE	SALT	FRESH	GRASS	DESERT	SCRUB	O WOODS	D WOODS	C WOODS	FARMS	TOWNS
Say's Phoebe	B					X		X				X	
Yellow-bellied Flycatcher	M								X	X	X		
Acadian Flycatcher	B								X	X			
Alder Flycatcher	M							X	X	X			
Willow Flycatcher	B							X	X	X			
Least Flycatcher	B							X	X	X		X	X
Eastern Wood Pewee	B								X	X	X	X	X
Olive-sided Flycatcher	M								X		X		

LARKS

	SEASON	OCEAN	SHORE	SALT	FRESH	GRASS	DESERT	SCRUB	O WOODS	D WOODS	C WOODS	FARMS	TOWNS
Horned Lark	R					X						X	

SWALLOWS

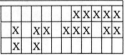

	SEASON	OCEAN	SHORE	SALT	FRESH	GRASS	DESERT	SCRUB	O WOODS	D WOODS	C WOODS	FARMS	TOWNS
Tree Swallow	B				X	X			X			X	
Bank Swallow	B				X	X						X	
Rough-winged Swallow	B				X							X	
Cliff Swallow	B				X	X						X	X
Barn Swallow	B				X	X						X	X
Purple Martin	B								X			X	X

JAYS & CROWS

	SEASON	OCEAN	SHORE	SALT	FRESH	GRASS	DESERT	SCRUB	O WOODS	D WOODS	C WOODS	FARMS	TOWNS
Blue Jay	R								X	X	X	X	X
Common Crow	R		X		X	X		X	X	X		X	X
Fish Crow	R		X		X								

	SEASON	OCEAN	SHORE	SALT	FRESH	GRASS	DESERT	SCRUB	O WOODS	D WOODS	C WOODS	FARMS	TOWNS
TITMICE													
Black-capped Chickadee	R							X	X	X	X	X	X
Carolina Chickadee	R								X	X		X	X
Boreal Chickadee	R										X		
Tufted Titmouse	R								X	X		X	X
BUSHTITS													
Common Bushtit	R							X	X	X		X	X
NUTHATCHES													
White-breasted Nuthatch	R								X	X	X	X	X
Red-breasted Nuthatch	W								X	X	X		X
CREEPERS													
Brown Creeper	R								X	X			
WRENS													
House Wren	B							X	X			X	X
Winter Wren	W							X		X	X		
Bewick's Wren	R							X	X			X	
Carolina Wren	R							X	X	X		X	X
Marsh Wren	B				X			X					
Sedge Wren	B				X	X							

<table>
	SEASON	OCEAN	SHORE	SALT	FRESH	GRASS	DESERT	SCRUB	O WOODS	D WOODS	C WOODS	FARMS	TOWNS

THRASHERS

	SEASON	OCEAN	SHORE	SALT	FRESH	GRASS	DESERT	SCRUB	O WOODS	D WOODS	C WOODS	FARMS	TOWNS
Mockingbird	R							X	X			X	X
Catbird	B							X	X	X		X	X
Brown Thrasher	B							X	X			X	X

THRUSHES

	SEASON	OCEAN	SHORE	SALT	FRESH	GRASS	DESERT	SCRUB	O WOODS	D WOODS	C WOODS	FARMS	TOWNS
American Robin	R							X	X			X	X
Wood Thrush	B								X	X			X
Hermit Thrush	M								X	X	X		
Swainson's Thrush	M								X	X	X		
Gray-cheeked Thrush	M								X	X	X		
Veery	B								X	X			
Eastern Bluebird	R					X			X			X	X
Blue-gray Gnatcatcher	B							X	X	X			
Golden-crowned Kinglet	W										X		
Ruby-crowned Kinglet	M							X		X	X		

PIPITS

	SEASON	OCEAN	SHORE	SALT	FRESH	GRASS	DESERT	SCRUB	O WOODS	D WOODS	C WOODS	FARMS	TOWNS
Water Pipit	M					X						X	
Sprague's Pipit	B					X						X	

WAXWINGS

	SEASON	OCEAN	SHORE	SALT	FRESH	GRASS	DESERT	SCRUB	O WOODS	D WOODS	C WOODS	FARMS	TOWNS
Bohemian Waxwing	W							X	X	X	X	X	X
Cedar Waxwing	R							X	X	X	X	X	X

SHRIKES

	SEASON	OCEAN	SHORE	SALT	FRESH	GRASS	DESERT	SCRUB	O WOODS	D WOODS	C WOODS	FARMS	TOWNS
Northern Shrike	W					X		X	X			X	
Loggerhead Shrike	B					X		X	X			X	
</table>

	SEASON	OCEAN	SHORE	SALT	FRESH	GRASS	DESERT	SCRUB	O WOODS	D WOODS	C WOODS	FARMS	TOWNS

STARLINGS

	SEASON	OCEAN	SHORE	SALT	FRESH	GRASS	DESERT	SCRUB	O WOODS	D WOODS	C WOODS	FARMS	TOWNS
Starling	R											X	X

VIREOS

	SEASON	OCEAN	SHORE	SALT	FRESH	GRASS	DESERT	SCRUB	O WOODS	D WOODS	C WOODS	FARMS	TOWNS
Solitary Vireo	B								X	X			
White-eyed Vireo	B							X				X	
Bell's Vireo	B							X					
Yellow-throated Vireo	B								X	X		X	X
Red-eyed Vireo	B								X	X		X	X
Warbling Vireo	B								X	X		X	X

WARBLERS

	SEASON	OCEAN	SHORE	SALT	FRESH	GRASS	DESERT	SCRUB	O WOODS	D WOODS	C WOODS	FARMS	TOWNS
Black-and-white Warbler	B								X	X			
Prothonotary Warbler	B				X				X	X			
Swainson's Warbler	B				X			X	X				
Worm-eating Warbler	B							X	X	X			
Golden-winged Warbler	B							X	X			X	
Blue-winged Warbler	B							X	X			X	
Tennessee Warbler	M							X	X	X	X		
Orange-crowned Warbler	M							X	X	X			
Nashville Warbler	M							X	X	X	X		
Northern Parula	B							X	X	X	X	X	
Yellow Warbler	B				X			X	X			X	
Magnolia Warbler	M							X	X	X	X		
Cape May Warbler	M								X	X	X		
Yellow-rumped Warbler	M							X	X	X	X		
Black-throated Green Warbler	B								X	X	X		
Black-throated Blue Warbler	M							X	X	X	X		
Cerulean Warbler	B								X	X			

WARBLERS, continued

	SEASON	OCEAN	SHORE	SALT	FRESH	GRASS	DESERT	SCRUB	O WOODS	D WOODS	C WOODS	FARMS	TOWNS
Yellow-throated Warbler	B								X	X	X		
Blackburnian Warbler	M								X	X	X		
Chestnut-sided Warbler	B							X	X	X		X	
Bay-breasted Warbler	M								X	X	X		
Blackpoll Warbler	M								X	X	X		
Pine Warbler	B										X		
Kirtland's Warbler	B										X		
Prairie Warbler	B							X	X	X	X		
Palm Warbler	M							X				X	
Ovenbird	B								X	X	X		
Northern Waterthrush	B				X				X	X	X		
Louisiana Waterthrush	B				X					X			
Common Yellowthroat	B							X	X			X	
Yellow-breasted Chat	B							X	X				
Kentucky Warbler	B									X			
Mourning Warbler	M							X		X			
Hooded Warbler	B									X			
Wilson's Warbler	M							X	X	X			
Canada Warbler	M							X	X	X	X		
American Redstart	B							X	X	X			

WEAVER FINCHES

	SEASON	OCEAN	SHORE	SALT	FRESH	GRASS	DESERT	SCRUB	O WOODS	D WOODS	C WOODS	FARMS	TOWNS
House Sparrow	R											X	X

BLACKBIRDS

	SEASON	OCEAN	SHORE	SALT	FRESH	GRASS	DESERT	SCRUB	O WOODS	D WOODS	C WOODS	FARMS	TOWNS
Bobolink	B				X	X						X	
Eastern Meadowlark	R					X						X	

BLACKBIRDS, *continued*

	SEASON	OCEAN	SHORE	SALT	FRESH	GRASS	DESERT	SCRUB	O WOODS	D WOODS	C WOODS	FARMS	TOWNS
Western Meadowlark	R					X						X	
Yellow-headed Blackbird	B				X	X						X	
Red-winged Blackbird	R				X	X						X	
Orchard Oriole	B							X				X	X
Northern Oriole	B								X	X		X	X
Rusty Blackbird	W				X			X	X	X	X		
Brewer's Blackbird	B					X						X	X
Great-tailed Grackle	R				X							X	X
Common Grackle	R								X			X	X
Brown-headed Cowbird	R								X			X	X

TANAGERS

	SEASON	OCEAN	SHORE	SALT	FRESH	GRASS	DESERT	SCRUB	O WOODS	D WOODS	C WOODS	FARMS	TOWNS
Scarlet Tanager	B								X	X			
Summer Tanager	B							X	X	X			

CARDINALS & BUNTINGS

	SEASON	OCEAN	SHORE	SALT	FRESH	GRASS	DESERT	SCRUB	O WOODS	D WOODS	C WOODS	FARMS	TOWNS
Cardinal	R							X	X			X	X
Rose-breasted Grosbeak	B							X	X	X		X	X
Blue Grosbeak	B							X				X	
Indigo Bunting	B							X	X			X	
Lazuli Bunting	B							X	X			X	
Dickcissel	B					X						X	

FINCHES

	SEASON	OCEAN	SHORE	SALT	FRESH	GRASS	DESERT	SCRUB	O WOODS	D WOODS	C WOODS	FARMS	TOWNS
Evening Grosbeak	W								X	X	X	X	X
Purple Finch	R									X	X	X	X
House Finch	R					X	X	X				X	X
Pine Grosbeak	W										X		
Common Redpoll	W					X		X				X	X

FINCHES, *continued*

	SEASON	OCEAN	SHORE	SALT	FRESH	GRASS	DESERT	SCRUB	O WOODS	D WOODS	C WOODS	FARMS	TOWNS
Pine Siskin	W								X	X	X		X
American Goldfinch	R							X	X			X	X
Red Crossbill	W										X		
White-winged Crossbill	W										X		

SPARROWS

	SEASON	OCEAN	SHORE	SALT	FRESH	GRASS	DESERT	SCRUB	O WOODS	D WOODS	C WOODS	FARMS	TOWNS
Rufous-sided Towhee	R							X	X			X	X
Savannah Sparrow	B					X						X	
Grasshopper Sparrow	B					X						X	
Lark Bunting	B					X						X	
Vesper Sparrow	B					X						X	
Lark Sparrow	B					X		X	X			X	
Dark-eyed Junco	W								X	X	X	X	X
Cassin's Sparrow	B					X							
Bachman's Sparrow	B							X	X		X		
Tree Sparrow	W					X		X	X			X	X
Chipping Sparrow	B					X		X	X			X	X
Clay-colored Sparrow	B					X		X					
Field Sparrow	R					X		X				X	
Harris' Sparrow	W							X	X				
White-crowned Sparrow	W					X		X	X			X	X
White-throated Sparrow	W							X	X	X	X	X	X
Fox Sparrow	W							X		X	X	X	
Lincoln's Sparrow	M				X			X	X	X		X	
Swamp Sparrow	R			X				X	X			X	

SPARROWS, continued

	SEASON	OCEAN	SHORE	SALT	FRESH	GRASS	DESERT	SCRUB	O WOODS	D WOODS	C WOODS	FARMS	TOWNS
Song Sparrow	R				X			X	X	X		X	X
McCown's Longspur	R					X						X	
Chestnut-collared Longspur	R					X						X	
Lapland Longspur	W					X						X	
Smith's Longspur	W					X						X	
Snow Bunting	W					X						X	

CHECKLIST OF TEXAS BIRDS

	SEASON	OCEAN	SHORE	SALT	FRESH	GRASS	DESERT	SCRUB	O WOODS	D WOODS	C WOODS	FARMS	TOWNS
LOONS													
Common Loon	W		X	X	X								
Red-throated Loon	W		X	X									
GREBES													
Horned Grebe	W		X	X									
Eared Grebe	R		X	X	X								
Pied-billed Grebe	R		X	X	X								
Least Grebe	R				X								
PELICANS													
White Pelican	R		X	X	X								
BOOBIES & GANNETS													
Brown Booby	M	X	X										
CORMORANTS													
Double-crested Cormorant	W		X	X	X								
Olivaceous Cormorant	R		X	X	X								

	SEASON	OCEAN	SHORE	SALT	FRESH	GRASS	DESERT	SCRUB	O WOODS	D WOODS	C WOODS	FARMS	TOWNS

ANHINGAS
	SEASON	OCEAN	SHORE	SALT	FRESH	GRASS	DESERT	SCRUB	O WOODS	D WOODS	C WOODS	FARMS	TOWNS
Anhinga	R				X								

HERONS & BITTERNS
	SEASON	OCEAN	SHORE	SALT	FRESH	GRASS	DESERT	SCRUB	O WOODS	D WOODS	C WOODS	FARMS	TOWNS
Great Blue Heron	R		X	X	X								
Green-backed Heron	B			X	X								
Cattle Egret	R			X	X	X						X	
Tricolored Heron	R		X	X	X								
Great Egret	R		X	X	X								
Snowy Egret	R		X	X	X								
Black-crowned Night-heron	R		X	X	X								
Yellow-crowned Night-heron	R			X	X								
American Bittern	R			X	X								
Least Bittern	R				X								

IBISES
	SEASON	OCEAN	SHORE	SALT	FRESH	GRASS	DESERT	SCRUB	O WOODS	D WOODS	C WOODS	FARMS	TOWNS
White-faced Ibis	R			X	X								
White Ibis	R			X	X								

GEESE
	SEASON	OCEAN	SHORE	SALT	FRESH	GRASS	DESERT	SCRUB	O WOODS	D WOODS	C WOODS	FARMS	TOWNS
Canada Goose	W			X	X	X						X	
White-fronted Goose	W			X	X	X							
Snow Goose	W			X	X	X							

MARSH DUCKS
	SEASON	OCEAN	SHORE	SALT	FRESH	GRASS	DESERT	SCRUB	O WOODS	D WOODS	C WOODS	FARMS	TOWNS
Mallard	W			X	X	X							

	SEASON	OCEAN	SHORE	SALT	FRESH	GRASS	DESERT	SCRUB	O WOODS	D WOODS	C WOODS	FARMS	TOWNS

MARSH DUCKS, *continued*

	SEASON	OCEAN	SHORE	SALT	FRESH	GRASS	DESERT	SCRUB	O WOODS	D WOODS	C WOODS	FARMS	TOWNS
Black Duck	W				X	X							
Mottled Duck	R		X	X	X								
Pintail	R				X	X							
Gadwall	W				X	X	X						
Northern Shoveler	W				X	X							
Blue-winged Teal	W				X	X							
Green-winged Teal	W				X	X							
Wood Duck	R				X								

WHISTLING DUCKS

	SEASON	OCEAN	SHORE	SALT	FRESH	GRASS	DESERT	SCRUB	O WOODS	D WOODS	C WOODS	FARMS	TOWNS
Fulvous Whistling Duck	R				X	X						X	
Black-bellied Whistling Duck	R				X							X	

DIVING DUCKS

	SEASON	OCEAN	SHORE	SALT	FRESH	GRASS	DESERT	SCRUB	O WOODS	D WOODS	C WOODS	FARMS	TOWNS
Redhead	W		X	X	X								
Canvasback	W		X	X	X								
Ring-necked Duck	W			X	X								
Greater Scaup	W		X	X	X								
Lesser Scaup	W		X	X	X								
Common Goldeneye	W		X	X	X								
Bufflehead	W		X	X	X								

STIFF-TAILED DUCKS

	SEASON	OCEAN	SHORE	SALT	FRESH	GRASS	DESERT	SCRUB	O WOODS	D WOODS	C WOODS	FARMS	TOWNS
Ruddy Duck	R		X	X	X								
Masked Duck	B		X	X	X								

MERGANSERS

	SEASON	OCEAN	SHORE	SALT	FRESH	GRASS	DESERT	SCRUB	O WOODS	D WOODS	C WOODS	FARMS	TOWNS
Common Merganser	W				X								

MERGANSERS, *continued*

	SEASON	OCEAN	SHORE	SALT	FRESH	GRASS	DESERT	SCRUB	O WOODS	D WOODS	C WOODS	FARMS	TOWNS
Red-breasted Merganser	W	X	X	X									
Hooded Merganser	W			X	X								

VULTURES

	SEASON	OCEAN	SHORE	SALT	FRESH	GRASS	DESERT	SCRUB	O WOODS	D WOODS	C WOODS	FARMS	TOWNS
Turkey Vulture	R					X	X		X			X	
Black Vulture	R					X	X		X			X	

KITES

	SEASON	OCEAN	SHORE	SALT	FRESH	GRASS	DESERT	SCRUB	O WOODS	D WOODS	C WOODS	FARMS	TOWNS
White-tailed Kite	R					X		X					
Mississippi Kite	B							X	X	X		X	X

ACCIPITERS

	SEASON	OCEAN	SHORE	SALT	FRESH	GRASS	DESERT	SCRUB	O WOODS	D WOODS	C WOODS	FARMS	TOWNS
Cooper's Hawk	R								X	X	X	X	
Sharp-shinned Hawk	W								X	X	X	X	X

HARRIERS

	SEASON	OCEAN	SHORE	SALT	FRESH	GRASS	DESERT	SCRUB	O WOODS	D WOODS	C WOODS	FARMS	TOWNS
Northern Harrier	W			X	X	X						X	

BUTEOS

	SEASON	OCEAN	SHORE	SALT	FRESH	GRASS	DESERT	SCRUB	O WOODS	D WOODS	C WOODS	FARMS	TOWNS
Ferruginous Hawk	W					X		X					
Red-tailed Hawk	R					X		X	X	X		X	
Red-shouldered Hawk	R					X			X	X		X	
Swainson's Hawk	B					X						X	
Broad-winged Hawk	B							X	X	X			
Harris' Hawk	R						X	X	X				

	SEASON	OCEAN	SHORE	SALT	FRESH	GRASS	DESERT	SCRUB	O WOODS	D WOODS	C WOODS	FARMS	TOWNS

BUTEOS, *continued*

	SEASON	OCEAN	SHORE	SALT	FRESH	GRASS	DESERT	SCRUB	O WOODS	D WOODS	C WOODS	FARMS	TOWNS
Zone-tailed Hawk	B							X	X	X	X		
White-tailed Hawk	R					X	X	X					

EAGLES

	SEASON	OCEAN	SHORE	SALT	FRESH	GRASS	DESERT	SCRUB	O WOODS	D WOODS	C WOODS	FARMS	TOWNS
Golden Eagle	R					X	X	X	X				

CARACARAS

	SEASON	OCEAN	SHORE	SALT	FRESH	GRASS	DESERT	SCRUB	O WOODS	D WOODS	C WOODS	FARMS	TOWNS
Caracara	R					X	X	X					

FALCONS

	SEASON	OCEAN	SHORE	SALT	FRESH	GRASS	DESERT	SCRUB	O WOODS	D WOODS	C WOODS	FARMS	TOWNS
Prairie Falcon	R					X	X	X					
Peregrine Falcon	R		X		X	X	X						
Merlin	W		X	X	X	X			X	X			X	X
American Kestrel	R					X		X	X			X	

GROUSE

	SEASON	OCEAN	SHORE	SALT	FRESH	GRASS	DESERT	SCRUB	O WOODS	D WOODS	C WOODS	FARMS	TOWNS
Greater Prairie Chicken	R					X							
Lesser Prairie Chicken	R					X	X						

QUAIL & PHEASANTS

	SEASON	OCEAN	SHORE	SALT	FRESH	GRASS	DESERT	SCRUB	O WOODS	D WOODS	C WOODS	FARMS	TOWNS
Bobwhite	R					X		X	X			X	

TURKEYS

	SEASON	OCEAN	SHORE	SALT	FRESH	GRASS	DESERT	SCRUB	O WOODS	D WOODS	C WOODS	FARMS	TOWNS
Wild Turkey	R								X	X	X		

	SEASON	OCEAN	SHORE	SALT	FRESH	GRASS	DESERT	SCRUB	O WOODS	D WOODS	C WOODS	FARMS	TOWNS

CHACHALACAS

	SEASON	OCEAN	SHORE	SALT	FRESH	GRASS	DESERT	SCRUB	O WOODS	D WOODS	C WOODS	FARMS	TOWNS
Chachalaca	R							X	X				

CRANES

	SEASON	OCEAN	SHORE	SALT	FRESH	GRASS	DESERT	SCRUB	O WOODS	D WOODS	C WOODS	FARMS	TOWNS
Whooping Crane	W				X	X						X	
Sandhill Crane	W				X	X						X	

RAILS

	SEASON	OCEAN	SHORE	SALT	FRESH	GRASS	DESERT	SCRUB	O WOODS	D WOODS	C WOODS	FARMS	TOWNS
King Rail	R			X	X								
Clapper Rail	R			X									
Virginia Rail	W			X	X								
Sora	W			X	X								
Yellow Rail	W				X	X						X	
Black Rail	W			X	X								
Purple Gallinule	B				X								
Common Gallinule (Moorhen)	R				X								
American Coot	R			X	X							X	

OYSTERCATCHERS

	SEASON	OCEAN	SHORE	SALT	FRESH	GRASS	DESERT	SCRUB	O WOODS	D WOODS	C WOODS	FARMS	TOWNS
American Oystercatcher	R	X	X										

STILTS & AVOCETS

	SEASON	OCEAN	SHORE	SALT	FRESH	GRASS	DESERT	SCRUB	O WOODS	D WOODS	C WOODS	FARMS	TOWNS
American Avocet	R	X	X	X									
Black-necked Stilt	R	X	X	X	X								

	SEASON		OCEAN	SHORE	SALT	FRESH	GRASS	DESERT	SCRUB	O WOODS	D WOODS	C WOODS	FARMS	TOWNS

PLOVERS

Semipalmated Plover	W		X	X	X									
Wilson's Plover	R		X	X	X									
Killdeer	R		X	X	X	X							X	
Piping Plover	W		X	X										
Snowy Plover	R		X	X	X									
Black-bellied Plover	W		X	X	X	X							X	

JACANAS

Northern Jacana	B					X								

GODWITS

Marbled Godwit	W		X	X	X	X								

CURLEWS

Whimbrel	W		X	X	X	X								
Long-billed Curlew	R		X	X	X	X								

UPLAND SANDPIPERS

Solitary Sandpiper	M					X								
Spotted Sandpiper	W		X	X	X	X								
Willet	R		X	X	X									
Greater Yellowlegs	W				X	X								
Lesser Yellowlegs	W			X	X	X								

	SEASON	OCEAN	SHORE	SALT	FRESH	GRASS	DESERT	SCRUB	O WOODS	D WOODS	C WOODS	FARMS	TOWNS

WOODCOCK

	SEASON	OCEAN	SHORE	SALT	FRESH	GRASS	DESERT	SCRUB	O WOODS	D WOODS	C WOODS	FARMS	TOWNS
Woodcock	W							X	X	X		X	

SNIPE

	SEASON	OCEAN	SHORE	SALT	FRESH	GRASS	DESERT	SCRUB	O WOODS	D WOODS	C WOODS	FARMS	TOWNS
Common Snipe	W			X	X	X							

SANDPIPERS

	SEASON	OCEAN	SHORE	SALT	FRESH	GRASS	DESERT	SCRUB	O WOODS	D WOODS	C WOODS	FARMS	TOWNS
Short-billed Dowitcher	W		X	X	X								
Long-billed Dowitcher	W		X	X	X								
Red Knot	W		X	X	X								
Sanderling	W		X	X	X								
Semipalmated Sandpiper	M		X	X	X								
Western Sandpiper	W		X	X	X								
Least Sandpiper	W		X	X	X								
Ruddy Turnstone	W		X	X									
Dunlin	W		X										

GULLS

	SEASON	OCEAN	SHORE	SALT	FRESH	GRASS	DESERT	SCRUB	O WOODS	D WOODS	C WOODS	FARMS	TOWNS
Herring Gull	W		X	X	X								X
Ring-billed Gull	W		X	X	X							X	X
Laughing Gull	R		X	X								X	X
Bonaparte's Gull	W		X	X	X								X

TERNS

	SEASON	OCEAN	SHORE	SALT	FRESH	GRASS	DESERT	SCRUB	O WOODS	D WOODS	C WOODS	FARMS	TOWNS
Gull-billed Tern	B		X	X	X							X	
Forster's Tern	R		X	X	X								

TERNS, *continued*

	SEASON	OCEAN	SHORE	SALT	FRESH	GRASS	DESERT	SCRUB	O WOODS	D WOODS	C WOODS	FARMS	TOWNS
Common Tern	M		X	X	X								
Least Tern	B		X	X	X								
Royal Tern	R		X	X									
Sandwich Tern	R		X	X	X								
Caspian Tern	R		X	X	X								
Black Tern	M		X	X	X							X	

SKIMMERS

	SEASON	OCEAN	SHORE	SALT	FRESH	GRASS	DESERT	SCRUB	O WOODS	D WOODS	C WOODS	FARMS	TOWNS
Black Skimmer	R		X	X									

PIGEONS & DOVES

	SEASON	OCEAN	SHORE	SALT	FRESH	GRASS	DESERT	SCRUB	O WOODS	D WOODS	C WOODS	FARMS	TOWNS
Band-tailed Pigeon	R									X	X		
Rock Dove	R											X	X
White-winged Dove	B					X	X	X				X	X
Mourning Dove	R					X	X	X				X	X
Ground Dove	R					X	X	X				X	X
Inca Dove	R					X	X	X				X	X
White-tipped Dove	R							X		X			

CUCKOOS

	SEASON	OCEAN	SHORE	SALT	FRESH	GRASS	DESERT	SCRUB	O WOODS	D WOODS	C WOODS	FARMS	TOWNS
Yellow-billed Cuckoo	B							X	X	X		X	
Roadrunner	R						X	X					
Groove-billed Ani	B							X				X	

OWLS

	SEASON	OCEAN	SHORE	SALT	FRESH	GRASS	DESERT	SCRUB	O WOODS	D WOODS	C WOODS	FARMS	TOWNS
Barn Owl	R					X		X	X			X	X
Eastern Screech Owl	R								X	X		X	X

OWLS, *continued*

	SEASON	OCEAN	SHORE	SALT	FRESH	GRASS	DESERT	SCRUB	O WOODS	D WOODS	C WOODS	FARMS	TOWNS
Western Screech Owl	R								X	X		X	X
Great Horned Owl	R				X	X	X	X	X	X	X	X	X
Burrowing Owl	R					X	X	X				X	
Barred Owl	R								X	X	X		
Long-eared Owl	R						X	X	X	X	X		
Short-eared Owl	W			X	X	X						X	
Elf Owl	R						X	X	X				

GOATSUCKERS

	SEASON	OCEAN	SHORE	SALT	FRESH	GRASS	DESERT	SCRUB	O WOODS	D WOODS	C WOODS	FARMS	TOWNS
Chuck-will's-widow	B								X	X	X	X	
Whip-poor-will	B								X	X		X	
Poor-will	B					X	X	X	X				
Common Nighthawk	B								X	X		X	X
Lesser Nighthawk	B					X	X	X				X	
Common Pauraque	R							X	X	X			

SWIFTS

	SEASON	OCEAN	SHORE	SALT	FRESH	GRASS	DESERT	SCRUB	O WOODS	D WOODS	C WOODS	FARMS	TOWNS
Chimney Swift	B								X			X	X
White-throated Swift	R						X	X	X			X	

HUMMINGBIRDS

	SEASON	OCEAN	SHORE	SALT	FRESH	GRASS	DESERT	SCRUB	O WOODS	D WOODS	C WOODS	FARMS	TOWNS
Ruby-throated Hummingbird	B								X	X	X	X	X
Broad-tailed Hummingbird	B								X	X	X	X	
Rufous Hummingbird	M								X	X	X		
Calliope Hummingbird	M								X	X	X	X	
Black-chinned Hummingbird	B								X	X		X	

HUMMINGBIRDS, *continued*

	SEASON	OCEAN	SHORE	SALT	FRESH	GRASS	DESERT	SCRUB	O WOODS	D WOODS	C WOODS	FARMS	TOWNS
Blue-throated Hummingbird	B								X	X	X		
Buff-bellied Hummingbird	B								X	X	X		

KINGFISHERS

	SEASON	OCEAN	SHORE	SALT	FRESH	GRASS	DESERT	SCRUB	O WOODS	D WOODS	C WOODS	FARMS	TOWNS
Belted Kingfisher	R		X	X	X								
Green Kingfisher	R				X								
Ringed Kingfisher	R				X								

WOODPECKERS

	SEASON	OCEAN	SHORE	SALT	FRESH	GRASS	DESERT	SCRUB	O WOODS	D WOODS	C WOODS	FARMS	TOWNS
Common Flicker	R							X	X	X	X	X	X
Pileated Woodpecker	R									X	X		
Red-bellied Woodpecker	R								X	X		X	X
Golden-fronted Woodpecker	R							X	X	X			X
Ladder-backed Woodpecker	R						X	X	X	X		X	X
Red-headed Woodpecker	R							X	X	X		X	X
Acorn Woodpecker	R								X	X	X		
Yellow-bellied Sapsucker	W								X	X		X	X
Hairy Woodpecker	R								X	X	X	X	X
Downy Woodpecker	R								X	X		X	X

FLYCATCHERS

	SEASON	OCEAN	SHORE	SALT	FRESH	GRASS	DESERT	SCRUB	O WOODS	D WOODS	C WOODS	FARMS	TOWNS
Eastern Kingbird	B					X			X	X		X	
Western Kingbird	B					X	X	X	X			X	
Cassin's Kingbird	B					X			X	X		X	
Couch's Kingbird	R								X	X			
Scissor-tailed Flycatcher	B					X			X	X		X	

FLYCATCHERS, *continued*

	SEASON	OCEAN	SHORE	SALT	FRESH	GRASS	DESERT	SCRUB	O WOODS	D WOODS	C WOODS	FARMS	TOWNS
Kiskadee Flycatcher	R					X		X	X			X	
Vermilion Flycatcher	R				X			X	X			X	
Great Crested Flycatcher	B							X	X	X			
Brown-crested Flycatcher	B							X	X	X			
Ash-throated Flycatcher	B						X	X	X	X		X	
Eastern Phoebe	R				X			X	X			X	X
Black Phoebe	R				X			X	X			X	X
Say's Phoebe	R					X	X	X				X	
Acadian Flycatcher	B								X	X			
Willow Flycatcher	M							X	X	X			
Dusky Flycatcher	M							X	X	X	X		
Western Flycatcher	B									X	X		
Eastern Wood Pewee	B								X	X	X		
Western Wood Pewee	B								X	X	X		
Olive-sided Flycatcher	M								X		X		

LARKS

	SEASON	OCEAN	SHORE	SALT	FRESH	GRASS	DESERT	SCRUB	O WOODS	D WOODS	C WOODS	FARMS	TOWNS
Horned Lark	R		X			X						X	

SWALLOWS

	SEASON	OCEAN	SHORE	SALT	FRESH	GRASS	DESERT	SCRUB	O WOODS	D WOODS	C WOODS	FARMS	TOWNS
Tree Swallow	W				X	X			X				
Bank Swallow	B				X	X						X	
Rough-winged Swallow	B				X			X				X	
Violet-green Swallow	B								X	X	X	X	X
Cliff Swallow	B				X	X		X				X	X
Cave Swallow	B					X	X	X					
Barn Swallow	B				X	X						X	X
Purple Martin	B								X			X	X

JAYS & CROWS

	SEASON	OCEAN	SHORE	SALT	FRESH	GRASS	DESERT	SCRUB	O WOODS	D WOODS	C WOODS	FARMS	TOWNS
Blue Jay	R								X	X	X	X	X
Scrub Jay	R							X	X	X			X
Brown Jay	R								X	X			
Gray-breasted Jay	R								X	X			
Pinyon Jay	W							X	X		X		
Green Jay	R							X	X	X			
Clark's Nutcracker	R										X		
Common Raven	R						X	X	X	X	X	X	X
Chihuahuan Raven	R					X	X	X	X			X	
Common Crow	R				X		X	X	X			X	X
Fish Crow	R		X	X	X								

TITMICE

	SEASON	OCEAN	SHORE	SALT	FRESH	GRASS	DESERT	SCRUB	O WOODS	D WOODS	C WOODS	FARMS	TOWNS
Mountain Chickadee	R										X		
Plain Titmouse	R								X	X		X	X
Tufted Titmouse	R								X	X	X	X	X

VERDINS

	SEASON	OCEAN	SHORE	SALT	FRESH	GRASS	DESERT	SCRUB	O WOODS	D WOODS	C WOODS	FARMS	TOWNS
Verdin	R						X	X					

BUSHTITS

	SEASON	OCEAN	SHORE	SALT	FRESH	GRASS	DESERT	SCRUB	O WOODS	D WOODS	C WOODS	FARMS	TOWNS
Common Bushtit	R							X	X	X	X		

NUTHATCHES

	SEASON	OCEAN	SHORE	SALT	FRESH	GRASS	DESERT	SCRUB	O WOODS	D WOODS	C WOODS	FARMS	TOWNS
White-breasted Nuthatch	B								X	X	X	X	X
Red-breasted Nuthatch	W								X	X	X		
Brown-headed Nuthatch	R								X	X			

CREEPERS

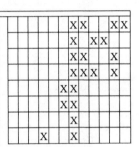

	Season	Ocean	Shore	Salt	Fresh	Grass	Desert	Scrub	O Woods	D Woods	C Woods	Farms	Towns
Brown Creeper	W									X	X		

WRENS

	Season	Ocean	Shore	Salt	Fresh	Grass	Desert	Scrub	O Woods	D Woods	C Woods	Farms	Towns
House Wren	W							X	X			X	X
Winter Wren	W								X	X	X		
Bewick's Wren	R							X	X			X	
Carolina Wren	R							X	X	X		X	
Cactus Wren	R						X	X					
Rock Wren	R						X	X					
Canyon Wren	R							X					
Marsh Wren	R				X			X					

THRASHERS

	Season	Ocean	Shore	Salt	Fresh	Grass	Desert	Scrub	O Woods	D Woods	C Woods	Farms	Towns
Mockingbird	R							X	X	X		X	X
Catbird	W								X	X	X	X	X
Brown Thrasher	W								X	X		X	X
Curve-billed Thrasher	R						X	X					
Long-billed Thrasher	R								X	X		X	X
Crissal Thrasher	R						X	X					
Sage Thrasher	W						X	X					

THRUSHES

	Season	Ocean	Shore	Salt	Fresh	Grass	Desert	Scrub	O Woods	D Woods	C Woods	Farms	Towns
American Robin	R							X	X			X	X
Wood Thrush	B								X	X			
Hermit Thrush	W								X	X	X		
Eastern Bluebird	R								X			X	

	SEASON	OCEAN	SHORE	SALT	FRESH	GRASS	DESERT	SCRUB	O WOODS	D WOODS	C WOODS	FARMS	TOWNS

THRUSHES, *continued*

	SEASON	OCEAN	SHORE	SALT	FRESH	GRASS	DESERT	SCRUB	O WOODS	D WOODS	C WOODS	FARMS	TOWNS
Western Bluebird	R								X			X	X
Mountain Bluebird	W				X			X				X	
Blue-gray Gnatcatcher	R							X	X	X			
Black-tailed Gnatcatcher	R						X	X					
Golden-crowned Kinglet	W										X		
Ruby-crowned Kinglet	W							X	X	X	X		

PIPITS

	SEASON	OCEAN	SHORE	SALT	FRESH	GRASS	DESERT	SCRUB	O WOODS	D WOODS	C WOODS	FARMS	TOWNS
Water Pipit	W		X			X						X	
Sprague's Pipit	W					X						X	

WAXWINGS

	SEASON	OCEAN	SHORE	SALT	FRESH	GRASS	DESERT	SCRUB	O WOODS	D WOODS	C WOODS	FARMS	TOWNS
Cedar Waxwing	W								X	X	X	X	X

SILKY-FLYCATCHERS

	SEASON	OCEAN	SHORE	SALT	FRESH	GRASS	DESERT	SCRUB	O WOODS	D WOODS	C WOODS	FARMS	TOWNS
Phainopepla	R							X	X				

SHRIKES

	SEASON	OCEAN	SHORE	SALT	FRESH	GRASS	DESERT	SCRUB	O WOODS	D WOODS	C WOODS	FARMS	TOWNS
Loggerhead Shrike	R					X	X	X	X			X	

STARLINGS

	SEASON	OCEAN	SHORE	SALT	FRESH	GRASS	DESERT	SCRUB	O WOODS	D WOODS	C WOODS	FARMS	TOWNS
Starling	R											X	X

VIREOS

	SEASON	OCEAN	SHORE	SALT	FRESH	GRASS	DESERT	SCRUB	O WOODS	D WOODS	C WOODS	FARMS	TOWNS
Black-capped Vireo	B							X	X	X			
Gray Vireo	B						X	X	X				
Solitary Vireo	B									X	X		
White-eyed Vireo	R							X	X			X	
Bell's Vireo	B							X					
Hutton's Vireo	R									X	X		
Yellow-throated Vireo	B								X	X		X	X
Warbling Vireo	B								X	X		X	X
Red-eyed Vireo	B								X	X		X	X

WARBLERS

	SEASON	OCEAN	SHORE	SALT	FRESH	GRASS	DESERT	SCRUB	O WOODS	D WOODS	C WOODS	FARMS	TOWNS
Black-and-white Warbler	W								X	X			X
Orange-crowned Warbler	W							X	X	X			
Nashville Warbler	M							X	X	X	X		
Lucy's Warbler	B						X	X					
Northern Parula	B							X	X	X			
Yellow Warbler	B				X			X	X			X	
Magnolia Warbler	M								X	X	X		
Yellow-rumped Warbler	W							X	X	X	X		
Townsend's Warbler	M										X		
Black-throated Green Warbler	W								X	X	X		
Golden-cheeked Warbler	B								X	X		X	
Black-throated Gray Warbler	M							X	X	X	X		
Cerulean Warbler	M								X	X			
Yellow-throated Warbler	R								X	X	X		
Pine Warbler	W										X		
Prairie Warbler	W							X	X		X		
Palm Warbler	W							X	X			X	

	SEASON	OCEAN	SHORE	SALT	FRESH	GRASS	DESERT	SCRUB	O WOODS	D WOODS	C WOODS	FARMS	TOWNS

WARBLERS, *continued*

	SEASON	OCEAN	SHORE	SALT	FRESH	GRASS	DESERT	SCRUB	O WOODS	D WOODS	C WOODS	FARMS	TOWNS
Northern Waterthrush	M				X				X	X			
Common Yellowthroat	R							X	X			X	
Yellow-breasted Chat	B							X	X			X	X
Kentucky Warbler	B									X			
MacGillivray's Warbler	M							X	X				
Hooded Warbler	B									X			
Wilson's Warbler	W							X	X	X			
American Redstart	W							X	X	X			
Painted Redstart	R									X	X		

WEAVER FINCHES

	SEASON	OCEAN	SHORE	SALT	FRESH	GRASS	DESERT	SCRUB	O WOODS	D WOODS	C WOODS	FARMS	TOWNS
House Sparrow	R											X	X

BLACKBIRDS

	SEASON	OCEAN	SHORE	SALT	FRESH	GRASS	DESERT	SCRUB	O WOODS	D WOODS	C WOODS	FARMS	TOWNS
Bobolink	M					X						X	
Eastern Meadowlark	R					X						X	
Western Meadowlark	R					X						X	
Yellow-headed Blackbird	R				X	X						X	
Red-winged Blackbird	R				X	X						X	
Orchard Oriole	B							X				X	X
Scott's Oriole	B						X	X	X				
Hooded Oriole	R							X				X	X
Northern Oriole	B								X	X		X	X
Altamira Oriole	R								X	X			
Audubon's Oriole	R									X			
Brewer's Blackbird	R					X						X	X
Boat-tailed Grackle	R		X	X								X	
Great-tailed Grackle	R		X	X			X					X	
Common Grackle	R				X	X		X	X	X		X	X

BLACKBIRDS, *continued*

	SEASON	OCEAN	SHORE	SALT	FRESH	GRASS	DESERT	SCRUB	O WOODS	D WOODS	C WOODS	FARMS	TOWNS
Brown-headed Cowbird	R											X	X
Bronzed Cowbird	R				X			X	X			X	

TANAGERS

	SEASON	OCEAN	SHORE	SALT	FRESH	GRASS	DESERT	SCRUB	O WOODS	D WOODS	C WOODS	FARMS	TOWNS
Western Tanager	B								X	X			
Summer Tanager	B							X	X	X			
Hepatic Tanager	B								X	X			

CARDINALS & BUNTINGS

	SEASON	OCEAN	SHORE	SALT	FRESH	GRASS	DESERT	SCRUB	O WOODS	D WOODS	C WOODS	FARMS	TOWNS
Cardinal	R							X	X			X	X
Pyrrhuloxia	R						X	X					
Rose-breasted Grosbeak	M							X	X	X		X	X
Blue Grosbeak	B							X				X	
Indigo Bunting	B							X	X			X	
Lazuli Bunting	M							X	X			X	
Painted Bunting	B							X	X				
Dickcissel	B					X						X	

FINCHES

	SEASON	OCEAN	SHORE	SALT	FRESH	GRASS	DESERT	SCRUB	O WOODS	D WOODS	C WOODS	FARMS	TOWNS
Evening Grosbeak	W								X	X	X	X	X
Purple Finch	W								X	X	X	X	X
House Finch	R						X	X	X			X	X
Pine Siskin	W									X	X		
American Goldfinch	W					X		X	X			X	X
Lesser Goldfinch	R					X		X	X			X	X

SPARROWS

	SEASON	OCEAN	SHORE	SALT	FRESH	GRASS	DESERT	SCRUB	O WOODS	D WOODS	C WOODS	FARMS	TOWNS
Green-tailed Towhee	W							X	X				

SPARROWS, *continued*

	SEASON	OCEAN	SHORE	SALT	FRESH	GRASS	DESERT	SCRUB	O WOODS	D WOODS	C WOODS	FARMS	TOWNS
Rufous-sided Towhee	W							X	X			X	X
Brown Towhee	R							X	X			X	X
Olive Sparrow	R					X		X	X				
Savannah Sparrow	W	X	X			X						X	
Grasshopper Sparrow	R					X						X	
Baird's Sparrow	W					X						X	
Henslow's Sparrow	W					X							
LeConte's Sparrow	W				X	X							
Seaside Sparrow	R			X									
Lark Bunting	W					X						X	
Vesper Sparrow	R					X						X	
Lark Sparrow	R					X	X	X	X			X	
Black-throated Sparrow	R						X						
Dark-eyed Junco	W								X	X	X	X	X
Rufous-crowned Sparrow	R							X	X				
Cassin's Sparrow	R					X	X	X					
Tree Sparrow	W					X		X	X			X	X
Chipping Sparrow	R					X		X	X			X	X
Clay-colored Sparrow	W					X		X				X	
Brewer's Sparrow	R					X	X	X					
Field Sparrow	R					X		X				X	
Black-chinned Sparrow	R						X	X					
Harris' Sparrow	W							X	X			X	X
White-crowned Sparrow	W							X	X			X	X
White-throated Sparrow	W							X		X	X	X	X
Fox Sparrow	W							X		X	X	X	
Lincoln's Sparrow	W				X			X	X	X		X	
Swamp Sparrow	W			X				X	X			X	X
Song Sparrow	W			X				X			X	X	X
McCown's Longspur	W					X						X	

	SEASON		OCEAN	SHORE	SALT	FRESH	GRASS	DESERT	SCRUB	O WOODS	D WOODS	C WOODS	FARMS	TOWNS
SPARROWS, *continued*														
Chestnut-collared Longspur	W						X						X	
Lapland Longspur	W			X		X	X						X	X

CHECKLIST OF BIRDS OF THE ROCKIES

	SEASON	OCEAN	SHORE	SALT	FRESH	GRASS	DESERT	SCRUB	O WOODS	D WOODS	C WOODS	FARMS	TOWNS

LOONS
Common Loon	M				X								

GREBES
Western Grebe	B				X								
Red-necked Grebe	M				X								
Horned Grebe	B				X								
Eared Grebe	B				X								
Pied-billed Grebe	B				X								

PELICANS
White Pelican	B				X								

CORMORANTS
Double-crested Cormorant	R				X								

HERONS & BITTERNS
Great Blue Heron	B				X								
Snowy Egret	B				X								
Black-crowned Night-heron	B				X								
American Bittern	B				X								

	SEASON	OCEAN	SHORE	SALT	FRESH	GRASS	DESERT	SCRUB	O WOODS	D WOODS	C WOODS	FARMS	TOWNS

SWANS
	SEASON	OCEAN	SHORE	SALT	FRESH	GRASS	DESERT	SCRUB	O WOODS	D WOODS	C WOODS	FARMS	TOWNS
Tundra Swan	M				X								
Trumpeter Swan	R				X								

GEESE
	SEASON	OCEAN	SHORE	SALT	FRESH	GRASS	DESERT	SCRUB	O WOODS	D WOODS	C WOODS	FARMS	TOWNS
Canada Goose	R				X							X	
Snow Goose	M				X								

MARSH DUCKS
	SEASON	OCEAN	SHORE	SALT	FRESH	GRASS	DESERT	SCRUB	O WOODS	D WOODS	C WOODS	FARMS	TOWNS
Mallard	R				X	X							
Pintail	B				X								
Gadwall	B				X								
American Wigeon	B				X								
Northern Shoveler	B				X								
Blue-winged Teal	B				X								
Cinnamon Teal	B				X								
Green-winged Teal	R				X								
Wood Duck	B				X								

DIVING DUCKS
	SEASON	OCEAN	SHORE	SALT	FRESH	GRASS	DESERT	SCRUB	O WOODS	D WOODS	C WOODS	FARMS	TOWNS
Redhead	B				X								
Canvasback	R				X								
Ring-necked Duck	B				X								
Greater Scaup	M				X								
Lesser Scaup	B				X								
Common Goldeneye	R				X								
Barrow's Goldeneye	R				X								
Bufflehead	R				X								

	SEASON	OCEAN	SHORE	SALT	FRESH	GRASS	DESERT	SCRUB	O WOODS	D WOODS	C WOODS	FARMS	TOWNS

DIVING DUCKS, *continued*

	SEASON	OCEAN	SHORE	SALT	FRESH	GRASS	DESERT	SCRUB	O WOODS	D WOODS	C WOODS	FARMS	TOWNS
Harlequin Duck	B				X								
White-winged Scoter	M				X								

STIFF-TAILED DUCKS

	SEASON	OCEAN	SHORE	SALT	FRESH	GRASS	DESERT	SCRUB	O WOODS	D WOODS	C WOODS	FARMS	TOWNS
Ruddy Duck	B				X								

MERGANSERS

	SEASON	OCEAN	SHORE	SALT	FRESH	GRASS	DESERT	SCRUB	O WOODS	D WOODS	C WOODS	FARMS	TOWNS
Common Merganser	R				X								
Red-breasted Merganser	M				X								
Hooded Merganser	B				X								

VULTURES

	SEASON	OCEAN	SHORE	SALT	FRESH	GRASS	DESERT	SCRUB	O WOODS	D WOODS	C WOODS	FARMS	TOWNS
Turkey Vulture	B					X	X		X			X	

ACCIPITERS

	SEASON	OCEAN	SHORE	SALT	FRESH	GRASS	DESERT	SCRUB	O WOODS	D WOODS	C WOODS	FARMS	TOWNS
Goshawk	R								X	X	X	X	
Cooper's Hawk	R								X	X	X	X	
Sharp-shinned Hawk	R									X	X	X	X

HARRIERS

	SEASON	OCEAN	SHORE	SALT	FRESH	GRASS	DESERT	SCRUB	O WOODS	D WOODS	C WOODS	FARMS	TOWNS
Northern Harrier	R					X	X					X	

	SEASON	OCEAN	SHORE	SALT	FRESH	GRASS	DESERT	SCRUB	O WOODS	D WOODS	C WOODS	FARMS	TOWNS
BUTEOS													
Rough-legged Hawk	W					X						X	
Ferruginous Hawk	R					X	X	X				X	
Red-tailed Hawk	R					X	X	X	X	X		X	
Swainson's Hawk	B					X	X					X	
EAGLES													
Golden Eagle	R					X	X	X	X				
Bald Eagle	W			X	X			X	X	X			
OSPREY													
Osprey	B				X								
FALCONS													
Prairie Falcon	R					X	X	X					
Peregrine Falcon	B			X	X							X	
Merlin	B			X	X					X			
American Kestrel	R					X			X	X		X	X
GROUSE													
Blue Grouse	R								X	X	X		
Spruce Grouse	R										X		
Ruffed Grouse	R								X	X	X		
Sharp-tailed Grouse	R					X		X	X				
Sage Grouse	R					X	X	X					
White-tailed Ptarmigan	R					X							

QUAIL & PHEASANTS

	SEASON	OCEAN	SHORE	SALT	FRESH	GRASS	DESERT	SCRUB	O WOODS	D WOODS	C WOODS	FARMS	TOWNS
Scaled Quail	R					X	X	X					
Ring-necked Pheasant	R					X		X				X	
Gray Partridge	R					X						X	
Chukar	R					X	X	X					

TURKEYS

	SEASON	OCEAN	SHORE	SALT	FRESH	GRASS	DESERT	SCRUB	O WOODS	D WOODS	C WOODS	FARMS	TOWNS
Wild Turkey	R								X	X	X	X	

CRANES

	SEASON	OCEAN	SHORE	SALT	FRESH	GRASS	DESERT	SCRUB	O WOODS	D WOODS	C WOODS	FARMS	TOWNS
Sandhill Crane	B				X	X						X	

RAILS

	SEASON	OCEAN	SHORE	SALT	FRESH	GRASS	DESERT	SCRUB	O WOODS	D WOODS	C WOODS	FARMS	TOWNS
Virginia Rail	B				X								
Sora	B				X							X	
American Coot	B				X							X	

STILTS & AVOCETS

	SEASON	OCEAN	SHORE	SALT	FRESH	GRASS	DESERT	SCRUB	O WOODS	D WOODS	C WOODS	FARMS	TOWNS
American Avocet	B				X								
Black-necked Stilt	B				X	X							

	SEASON	OCEAN	SHORE	SALT	FRESH	GRASS	DESERT	SCRUB	O WOODS	D WOODS	C WOODS	FARMS	TOWNS

PLOVERS

	SEASON	OCEAN	SHORE	SALT	FRESH	GRASS	DESERT	SCRUB	O WOODS	D WOODS	C WOODS	FARMS	TOWNS
Semipalmated Plover	M				X								
Killdeer	B					X						X	
Snowy Plover	B				X								
Black-bellied Plover	M				X	X						X	
Mountain Plover	B					X	X						

GODWITS

	SEASON	OCEAN	SHORE	SALT	FRESH	GRASS	DESERT	SCRUB	O WOODS	D WOODS	C WOODS	FARMS	TOWNS
Hudsonian Godwit	M				X	X							
Marbled Godwit	M				X	X							

CURLEWS

	SEASON	OCEAN	SHORE	SALT	FRESH	GRASS	DESERT	SCRUB	O WOODS	D WOODS	C WOODS	FARMS	TOWNS
Long-billed Curlew	B				X	X							

UPLAND SANDPIPERS

	SEASON	OCEAN	SHORE	SALT	FRESH	GRASS	DESERT	SCRUB	O WOODS	D WOODS	C WOODS	FARMS	TOWNS
Upland Sandpiper	B					X						X	
Solitary Sandpiper	M				X								
Spotted Sandpiper	B				X	X			X	X		X	
Willet	B				X								
Greater Yellowlegs	M				X	X					X	X	
Lesser Yellowlegs	M				X	X					X		

PHALAROPES

	SEASON	OCEAN	SHORE	SALT	FRESH	GRASS	DESERT	SCRUB	O WOODS	D WOODS	C WOODS	FARMS	TOWNS
Wilson's Phalarope	B				X	X							

	SEASON	OCEAN	SHORE	SALT	FRESH	GRASS	DESERT	SCRUB	O WOODS	D WOODS	C WOODS	FARMS	TOWNS

SNIPE

	SEASON	OCEAN	SHORE	SALT	FRESH	GRASS	DESERT	SCRUB	O WOODS	D WOODS	C WOODS	FARMS	TOWNS
Common Snipe	B				X	X							

SANDPIPERS

	SEASON	OCEAN	SHORE	SALT	FRESH	GRASS	DESERT	SCRUB	O WOODS	D WOODS	C WOODS	FARMS	TOWNS
Long-billed Dowitcher	M				X								
Sanderling	M				X								
Semipalmated Sandpiper	M				X								
Western Sandpiper	M				X								
Least Sandpiper	M				X								
Baird's Sandpiper	M				X								
Pectoral Sandpiper	M				X								

GULLS

	SEASON	OCEAN	SHORE	SALT	FRESH	GRASS	DESERT	SCRUB	O WOODS	D WOODS	C WOODS	FARMS	TOWNS
Herring Gull	W				X							X	X
California Gull	B				X	X							
Ring-billed Gull	B				X							X	X
Franklin's Gull	B				X	X						X	
Bonaparte's Gull	M				X								X

TERNS

	SEASON	OCEAN	SHORE	SALT	FRESH	GRASS	DESERT	SCRUB	O WOODS	D WOODS	C WOODS	FARMS	TOWNS
Forster's Tern	B				X								
Caspian Tern	B				X								
Black Tern	B				X								

PIGEONS & DOVES

	SEASON	OCEAN	SHORE	SALT	FRESH	GRASS	DESERT	SCRUB	O WOODS	D WOODS	C WOODS	FARMS	TOWNS
Band-tailed Pigeon	B										X	X	

PIGEONS & DOVES, *continued*

	SEASON	OCEAN	SHORE	SALT	FRESH	GRASS	DESERT	SCRUB	O WOODS	D WOODS	C WOODS	FARMS	TOWNS
Rock Dove	R											X	X
Mourning Dove	R					X	X	X				X	X

CUCKOOS

	SEASON	OCEAN	SHORE	SALT	FRESH	GRASS	DESERT	SCRUB	O WOODS	D WOODS	C WOODS	FARMS	TOWNS
Yellow-billed Cuckoo	B								X	X		X	

OWLS

	SEASON	OCEAN	SHORE	SALT	FRESH	GRASS	DESERT	SCRUB	O WOODS	D WOODS	C WOODS	FARMS	TOWNS
Barn Owl	R					X		X	X			X	X
Western Screech Owl	R								X	X		X	X
Great Horned Owl	R					X	X	X	X	X	X	X	X
Snowy Owl	W			X	X								
Burrowing Owl	B					X	X	X				X	
Spotted Owl	R										X		
Long-eared Owl	R						X	X	X	X	X		
Short-eared Owl	R		X	X		X							
Saw-whet Owl	R									X	X		
Pygmy Owl	R									X	X		

GOATSUCKERS

	SEASON	OCEAN	SHORE	SALT	FRESH	GRASS	DESERT	SCRUB	O WOODS	D WOODS	C WOODS	FARMS	TOWNS
Poor-will	B					X	X	X	X				
Common Nighthawk	B								X			X	X

SWIFTS

	SEASON	OCEAN	SHORE	SALT	FRESH	GRASS	DESERT	SCRUB	O WOODS	D WOODS	C WOODS	FARMS	TOWNS
Black Swift	B								X				
White-throated Swift	B						X	X	X	X	X	X	X

HUMMINGBIRDS

	SEASON	OCEAN	SHORE	SALT	FRESH	GRASS	DESERT	SCRUB	O WOODS	D WOODS	C WOODS	FARMS	TOWNS
Broad-tailed Hummingbird	B							X	X	X	X		X
Rufous Hummingbird	B								X	X	X		X
Calliope Hummingbird	B							X	X	X	X		
Black-chinned Hummingbird	B							X	X				X

KINGFISHERS

	SEASON	OCEAN	SHORE	SALT	FRESH	GRASS	DESERT	SCRUB	O WOODS	D WOODS	C WOODS	FARMS	TOWNS
Belted Kingfisher	B				X								

WOODPECKERS

	SEASON	OCEAN	SHORE	SALT	FRESH	GRASS	DESERT	SCRUB	O WOODS	D WOODS	C WOODS	FARMS	TOWNS
Common Flicker	R							X	X	X	X	X	X
Pileated Woodpecker	R								X	X			
Lewis' Woodpecker	R					X		X	X	X	X		
Yellow-bellied Sapsucker	B								X	X		X	
Williamson's Sapsucker	B								X		X		
Hairy Woodpecker	R								X	X		X	X
Downy Woodpecker	R								X	X		X	X
Three-toed Woodpecker	R										X		
Black-backed Woodpecker	R										X		

FLYCATCHERS

	SEASON	OCEAN	SHORE	SALT	FRESH	GRASS	DESERT	SCRUB	O WOODS	D WOODS	C WOODS	FARMS	TOWNS
Eastern Kingbird	B					X		X	X			X	X
Western Kingbird	B					X		X	X			X	
Cassin's Kingbird	B					X		X	X			X	
Ash-throated Flycatcher	B						X	X	X			X	
Say's Phoebe	B					X	X	X				X	
Willow Flycatcher	B							X	X	X			

FLYCATCHERS, *continued*

	SEASON	OCEAN	SHORE	SALT	FRESH	GRASS	DESERT	SCRUB	O WOODS	D WOODS	C WOODS	FARMS	TOWNS
Least Flycatcher	B								X	X			
Hammond's Flycatcher	B										X		
Dusky Flycatcher	B							X	X	X	X		
Gray Flycatcher	B						X	X	X				
Western Flycatcher	B									X	X		
Western Wood Pewee	B								X	X	X		
Olive-sided Flycatcher	B								X		X		

LARKS

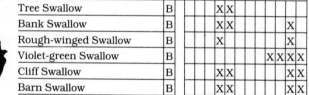

	SEASON	OCEAN	SHORE	SALT	FRESH	GRASS	DESERT	SCRUB	O WOODS	D WOODS	C WOODS	FARMS	TOWNS
Horned Lark	R					X	X					X	

SWALLOWS

	SEASON	OCEAN	SHORE	SALT	FRESH	GRASS	DESERT	SCRUB	O WOODS	D WOODS	C WOODS	FARMS	TOWNS
Tree Swallow	B			X	X								
Bank Swallow	B			X	X							X	
Rough-winged Swallow	B			X								X	
Violet-green Swallow	B									X	X	X	X
Cliff Swallow	B			X	X							X	X
Barn Swallow	B			X	X							X	X

JAYS & CROWS

	SEASON	OCEAN	SHORE	SALT	FRESH	GRASS	DESERT	SCRUB	O WOODS	D WOODS	C WOODS	FARMS	TOWNS
Steller's Jay	R								X	X	X		
Scrub Jay	R							X	X	X			X
Pinyon Jay	R							X	X		X		
Gray Jay	R										X		
Black-billed Magpie	R					X		X	X			X	X
Clark's Nutcracker	R										X		
Common Raven	R				X	X	X	X	X	X	X	X	
Common Crow	R					X		X	X	X		X	X

	SEASON	OCEAN	SHORE	SALT	FRESH	GRASS	DESERT	SCRUB	O WOODS	D WOODS	C WOODS	FARMS	TOWNS
TITMICE													
Black-capped Chickadee	R							X	X	X	X	X	X
Mountain Chickadee	R										X		
Plain Titmouse	R							X					
BUSHTITS													
Common Bushtit	R							X	X	X		X	X
DIPPERS													
Dipper	B				X								
NUTHATCHES													
White-breasted Nuthatch	B								X	X	X	X	X
Red-breasted Nuthatch	R								X		X		
Pygmy Nuthatch	R										X		
CREEPERS													
Brown Creeper	R									X	X		
WRENS													
House Wren	B							X	X			X	X
Bewick's Wren	R							X	X			X	
Winter Wren	B								X		X	X	
Rock Wren	B						X	X					

	SEASON	OCEAN	SHORE	SALT	FRESH	GRASS	DESERT	SCRUB	O WOODS	D WOODS	C WOODS	FARMS	TOWNS
WRENS, *continued*													
Canyon Wren	R						X						
Marsh Wren	B				X		X						
THRASHERS													
Mockingbird	B							X	X			X	X
Catbird	B							X	X	X		X	X
Sage Thrasher	B						X	X					
THRUSHES													
American Robin	R							X	X			X	X
Hermit Thrush	B								X	X			
Swainson's Thrush	B								X	X			
Gray-cheeked Thrush	M								X	X			
Veery	B							X	X	X			
Western Bluebird	R								X			X	
Mountain Bluebird	R					X		X	X			X	
Townsend's Solitaire	R								X		X		
Blue-gray Gnatcatcher	B						X	X	X				
Golden-crowned Kinglet	R										X		
Ruby-crowned Kinglet	B									X	X		
PIPITS													
Water Pipit	B				X							X	X
WAXWINGS													
Bohemian Waxwing	W							X	X	X	X	X	X
Cedar Waxwing	B							X	X	X	X	X	X

	SEASON	OCEAN	SHORE	SALT	FRESH	GRASS	DESERT	SCRUB	O WOODS	D WOODS	C WOODS	FARMS	TOWNS
SHRIKES													
Northern Shrike	W					X		X	X			X	
Loggerhead Shrike	R					X	X	X	X			X	
STARLINGS													
Starling	R											X	X
VIREOS													
Solitary Vireo	B								X	X			
Red-eyed Vireo	B								X	X		X	X
Warbling Vireo	B								X	X		X	X
WARBLERS													
Orange-crowned Warbler	B							X	X	X	X		
Nashville Warbler	B							X	X	X	X		
Virginia's Warbler	B							X	X	X	X		
Yellow Warbler	B				X			X	X			X	
Yellow-rumped Warbler	B							X	X	X	X		
Townsend's Warbler	B										X		
Black-throated Gray Warbler	B							X	X	X	X		
Blackpoll Warbler	M								X	X	X		
Northern Waterthrush	M				X				X	X			
Common Yellowthroat	B				X			X	X			X	X
Yellow-breasted Chat	B							X	X				
MacGillivray's Warbler	B							X	X				
Wilson's Warbler	B							X	X	X			
American Redstart	B							X		X			
WEAVER FINCHES													
House Sparrow	R											X	X

	SEASON	OCEAN	SHORE	SALT	FRESH	GRASS	DESERT	SCRUB	O WOODS	D WOODS	C WOODS	FARMS	TOWNS
BLACKBIRDS													
Bobolink	B					X						X	
Western Meadowlark	R					X						X	
Yellow-headed Blackbird	B				X							X	
Red-winged Blackbird	R				X	X						X	
Northern Oriole	B								X	X		X	X
Brewer's Blackbird	R					X		X				X	X
Brown-headed Cowbird	B							X	X			X	X
TANAGERS													
Western Tanager	B								X	X			
CARDINALS & BUNTINGS													
Black-headed Grosbeak	B								X	X		X	
Indigo Bunting	B								X	X		X	
Lazuli Bunting	B							X	X	X		X	
FINCHES													
Evening Grosbeak	R								X	X	X	X	X
Cassin's Finch	R										X		
House Finch	R					X	X	X				X	X
Pine Grosbeak	R										X		
Rosy Finch	R				X								
Hoary Redpoll	W					X	X					X	X
Common Redpoll	W					X	X					X	X
Pine Siskin	R								X	X	X		
American Goldfinch	B					X		X	X			X	X
Lesser Goldfinch	R					X		X	X			X	X
Red Crossbill	R										X		
White-winged Crossbill	R										X		

SPARROWS

	SEASON	OCEAN	SHORE	SALT	FRESH	GRASS	DESERT	SCRUB	O WOODS	D WOODS	C WOODS	FARMS	TOWNS
Green-tailed Towhee	B							X	X				
Rufous-sided Towhee	R							X	X			X	X
Savannah Sparrow	B					X						X	
Grasshopper Sparrow	B					X							
Baird's Sparrow	B					X						X	
Vesper Sparrow	B					X	X					X	
Lark Sparrow	B					X		X	X			X	
Black-throated Sparrow	B						X						
Sage Sparrow	R						X	X					
Dark-eyed Junco	R								X	X	X	X	X
Tree Sparrow	W							X	X			X	X
Chipping Sparrow	B							X	X			X	X
Brewer's Sparrow	B					X	X	X				X	
White-crowned Sparrow	R							X	X			X	X
White-throated Sparrow	M							X	X	X	X	X	X
Fox Sparrow	B							X		X	X	X	
Lincoln's Sparrow	B					X		X	X	X			
Song Sparrow	R			X				X				X	X
Lapland Longspur	W					X						X	X
Snow Bunting	W					X						X	

CHECKLIST OF NORTHWESTERN BIRDS

	SEASON	OCEAN	SHORE	SALT	FRESH	GRASS	DESERT	SCRUB	O WOODS	D WOODS	C WOODS	FARMS	TOWNS
LOONS													
Common Loon	R	X	X	X	X								
Red-throated Loon	W		X	X	X								
GREBES													
Western Grebe	R			X	X								
Red-necked Grebe	R		X	X	X								
Horned Grebe	R		X	X	X								
Eared Grebe	R		X	X	X								
Pied-billed Grebe	R		X	X	X								
SHEARWATERS													
Pink-footed Shearwater	M	X											
Sooty Shearwater	M	X											
Short-tailed Shearwater	M	X											
Buller's Shearwater	M	X	X										
STORM-PETRELS													
Fork-tailed Storm-petrel	R	X	X	X									
Leach's Storm-petrel	B	X	X										
PELICANS													
Brown Pelican	M	X	X	X									
White Pelican	B		X	X	X								

	SEASON	OCEAN	SHORE	SALT	FRESH	GRASS	DESERT	SCRUB	O WOODS	D WOODS	C WOODS	FARMS	TOWNS

CORMORANTS

	SEASON	OCEAN	SHORE	SALT	FRESH	GRASS	DESERT	SCRUB	O WOODS	D WOODS	C WOODS	FARMS	TOWNS
Brandt's Cormorant	R		X	X									
Double-crested Cormorant	R		X	X	X								
Pelagic Cormorant	R	X	X	X									

HERONS & BITTERNS

	SEASON	OCEAN	SHORE	SALT	FRESH	GRASS	DESERT	SCRUB	O WOODS	D WOODS	C WOODS	FARMS	TOWNS
Great Blue Heron	R			X	X								
Green-backed Heron	B			X	X								
Cattle Egret	B			X	X	X						X	
Great Egret	R			X	X								
Snowy Egret	B			X	X							X	
Black-crowned Night-heron	R			X	X								
American Bittern	R			X	X								
Least Bittern	B				X								

SWANS

	SEASON	OCEAN	SHORE	SALT	FRESH	GRASS	DESERT	SCRUB	O WOODS	D WOODS	C WOODS	FARMS	TOWNS
Tundra Swan	M			X	X	X							
Trumpeter Swan	R			X	X	X							

GEESE

	SEASON	OCEAN	SHORE	SALT	FRESH	GRASS	DESERT	SCRUB	O WOODS	D WOODS	C WOODS	FARMS	TOWNS
Canada Goose	R			X	X	X						X	
Brant	W	X	X										
White-fronted Goose	W				X	X							
Snow Goose	W		X	X	X	X							

MARSH DUCKS

	SEASON	OCEAN	SHORE	SALT	FRESH	GRASS	DESERT	SCRUB	O WOODS	D WOODS	C WOODS	FARMS	TOWNS
Mallard	R			X	X	X							
Pintail	R			X	X								
Gadwall	R			X	X	X							
American Wigeon	R			X	X	X							

MARSH DUCKS, *continued*

	SEASON	OCEAN	SHORE	SALT	FRESH	GRASS	DESERT	SCRUB	O WOODS	D WOODS	C WOODS	FARMS	TOWNS
Northern Shoveler	R			X	X								
Blue-winged Teal	B			X	X	X							
Cinnamon Teal	R				X								
Green-winged Teal	R			X	X								
Wood Duck	R				X								

DIVING DUCKS

	SEASON	OCEAN	SHORE	SALT	FRESH	GRASS	DESERT	SCRUB	O WOODS	D WOODS	C WOODS	FARMS	TOWNS
Redhead	B			X	X								
Canvasback	R			X	X								
Ring-necked Duck	R			X	X								
Tufted Duck	W			X	X								
Greater Scaup	W		X	X	X								
Lesser Scaup	R		X	X	X								
Common Goldeneye	R		X	X	X								
Barrow's Goldeneye	R		X	X	X								
Bufflehead	W		X	X	X								
Harlequin Duck	R		X	X	X								
Oldsquaw	W	X	X	X	X	X	X						
Black Scoter	W	X	X	X	X								
White-winged Scoter	R		X	X	X								
Surf Scoter	W	X	X	X	X								

STIFF-TAILED DUCKS

	SEASON	OCEAN	SHORE	SALT	FRESH	GRASS	DESERT	SCRUB	O WOODS	D WOODS	C WOODS	FARMS	TOWNS
Ruddy Duck	R		X	X	X								

MERGANSERS

	SEASON	OCEAN	SHORE	SALT	FRESH	GRASS	DESERT	SCRUB	O WOODS	D WOODS	C WOODS	FARMS	TOWNS
Common Merganser	R			X	X								
Red-breasted Merganser	W		X	X	X								
Hooded Merganser	R			X	X								

	SEASON	OCEAN	SHORE	SALT	FRESH	GRASS	DESERT	SCRUB	O WOODS	D WOODS	C WOODS	FARMS	TOWNS
VULTURES													
Turkey Vulture	R					X	X		X			X	
ACCIPITERS													
Goshawk	R								X	X	X	X	
Cooper's Hawk	R								X	X	X	X	
Sharp-shinned Hawk	R									X	X	X	
HARRIERS													
Northern Harrier	R				X	X						X	
BUTEOS													
Rough-legged Hawk	W					X		X				X	
Ferruginous Hawk	R					X		X					
Red-tailed Hawk	R					X		X	X	X		X	
Swainson's Hawk	B				X	X						X	
EAGLES													
Golden Eagle	R					X	X	X	X				
Bald Eagle	R		X	X	X								
OSPREY													
Osprey	B		X	X	X								

FALCONS

	SEASON	OCEAN	SHORE	SALT	FRESH	GRASS	DESERT	SCRUB	O WOODS	D WOODS	C WOODS	FARMS	TOWNS
Peregrine Falcon	R		X			X	X						
Merlin	R		X			X				X	X		
American Kestrel	R					X		X	X			X	

GROUSE

	SEASON	OCEAN	SHORE	SALT	FRESH	GRASS	DESERT	SCRUB	O WOODS	D WOODS	C WOODS	FARMS	TOWNS
Blue Grouse	R								X	X	X		
Spruce Grouse	R										X		
Ruffed Grouse	R								X	X	X	X	
Sharp-tailed Grouse	R					X		X	X				
Sage Grouse	R					X	X	X					
White-tailed Ptarmigan	R					X							

QUAIL & PHEASANTS

	SEASON	OCEAN	SHORE	SALT	FRESH	GRASS	DESERT	SCRUB	O WOODS	D WOODS	C WOODS	FARMS	TOWNS
California Quail	R					X	X	X				X	X
Gambel's Quail	R						X	X					
Mountain Quail	R							X	X	X	X		
Ring-necked Pheasant	R					X		X				X	
Gray Partridge	R					X						X	
Chukar	R					X	X	X					

CRANES

	SEASON	OCEAN	SHORE	SALT	FRESH	GRASS	DESERT	SCRUB	O WOODS	D WOODS	C WOODS	FARMS	TOWNS
Sandhill Crane	B				X	X						X	

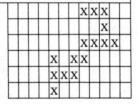

	SEASON	OCEAN	SHORE	SALT	FRESH	GRASS	DESERT	SCRUB	O WOODS	D WOODS	C WOODS	FARMS	TOWNS

RAILS

	SEASON	OCEAN	SHORE	SALT	FRESH	GRASS	DESERT	SCRUB	O WOODS	D WOODS	C WOODS	FARMS	TOWNS
Virginia Rail	R			X	X								
Sora	B			X	X							X	
Yellow Rail	R				X	X						X	
American Coot	R				X							X	

OYSTERCATCHERS

	SEASON	OCEAN	SHORE	SALT	FRESH	GRASS	DESERT	SCRUB	O WOODS	D WOODS	C WOODS	FARMS	TOWNS
Black Oystercatcher	R	X	X										

STILTS & AVOCETS

	SEASON	OCEAN	SHORE	SALT	FRESH	GRASS	DESERT	SCRUB	O WOODS	D WOODS	C WOODS	FARMS	TOWNS
American Avocet	B	X	X	X									
Black-necked Stilt	B	X	X	X	X								

PLOVERS

	SEASON	OCEAN	SHORE	SALT	FRESH	GRASS	DESERT	SCRUB	O WOODS	D WOODS	C WOODS	FARMS	TOWNS
Semipalmated Plover	M	X	X	X									
Killdeer	R	X	X	X	X							X	
Snowy Plover	B	X	X	X									
Black-bellied Plover	W	X	X	X	X							X	

GODWITS

	SEASON	OCEAN	SHORE	SALT	FRESH	GRASS	DESERT	SCRUB	O WOODS	D WOODS	C WOODS	FARMS	TOWNS
Marbled Godwit	M	X	X	X	X								

CURLEWS

	SEASON	OCEAN	SHORE	SALT	FRESH	GRASS	DESERT	SCRUB	O WOODS	D WOODS	C WOODS	FARMS	TOWNS
Whimbrel	M	X	X	X	X								
Long-billed Curlew	B	X	X	X	X								

	SEASON	OCEAN	SHORE	SALT	FRESH	GRASS	DESERT	SCRUB	O WOODS	D WOODS	C WOODS	FARMS	TOWNS
UPLAND SANDPIPERS													
Upland Sandpiper	B					X						X	
Solitary Sandpiper	M				X								
Spotted Sandpiper	R		X	X	X	X							
Willet	R		X	X	X								
Greater Yellowlegs	W				X	X							
Lesser Yellowlegs	M			X	X	X							
PHALAROPES													
Red Phalarope	M	X	X										
Red-necked Phalarope	M	X	X		X	X							
SNIPE													
Common Snipe	R			X	X	X							
SANDPIPERS													
Short-billed Dowitcher	M		X	X	X								
Long-billed Dowitcher	W			X	X								
Red Knot	M		X	X	X								
Sanderling	W		X	X	X								
Western Sandpiper	W		X	X	X								
Least Sandpiper	W		X	X	X								
Black Turnstone	W		X	X									
Ruddy Turnstone	M		X	X									
Surfbird	W		X	X									
Rock Sandpiper	W		X										
Dunlin	W		X										

	SEASON	OCEAN	SHORE	SALT	FRESH	GRASS	DESERT	SCRUB	O WOODS	D WOODS	C WOODS	FARMS	TOWNS
GULLS													
Glaucous-winged Gull	R	X	X	X									X
Western Gull	R	X	X	X									X
Herring Gull	W		X	X	X	X						X	X
California Gull	R		X	X	X	X							
Ring-billed Gull	R		X	X	X							X	X
Mew Gull	W		X	X	X								
Heermann's Gull	W	X	X	X									
Bonaparte's Gull	W		X	X	X								X
Black-legged Kittiwake	W	X	X										
TERNS													
Forster's Tern	B			X	X								
Common Tern	M		X	X	X								
Caspian Tern	B		X	X	X								
Black Tern	B		X	X	X							X	
ALCIDS													
Common Murre	R	X	X										
Pigeon Guillemot	R		X	X									
Tufted Puffin	R	X	X										
Rhinoceros Auklet	R	X	X										
Cassin's Auklet	R	X	X										
Marbled Murrelet	R		X	X							X		
PIGEONS & DOVES													
Band-tailed Pigeon	B									X	X		
Rock Dove	R											X	X
Mourning Dove	R					X	X	X				X	X

	SEASON	OCEAN	SHORE	SALT	FRESH	GRASS	DESERT	SCRUB	O WOODS	D WOODS	C WOODS	FARMS	TOWNS
OWLS													
Barn Owl	R					X		X	X			X	X
Western Screech Owl	R								X	X		X	X
Great Horned Owl	R					X	X	X	X	X	X	X	X
Burrowing Owl	B		X			X	X	X				X	X
Barred Owl	R									X	X		
Spotted Owl	R										X		
Long-eared Owl	R						X	X	X	X	X		
Short-eared Owl	R			X	X			X				X	
Saw-whet Owl	R									X	X		
Pygmy Owl	R									X	X		
GOATSUCKERS													
Poor-will	B					X	X	X	X				
Common Nighthawk	B					X			X			X	X
SWIFTS													
Vaux's Swift	B									X	X		
White-throated Swift	B						X	X	X	X	X	X	
HUMMINGBIRDS													
Rufous Hummingbird	B					X			X	X	X		
Allen's Hummingbird	B					X		X	X				
Calliope Hummingbird	B					X		X	X	X	X		
Anna's Hummingbird	R							X	X			X	X
Black-chinned Hummingbird	B					X		X	X			X	
KINGFISHERS													
Belted Kingfisher	R		X	X	X								

	SEASON	OCEAN	SHORE	SALT	FRESH	GRASS	DESERT	SCRUB	O WOODS	D WOODS	C WOODS	FARMS	TOWNS

WOODPECKERS

	SEASON	OCEAN	SHORE	SALT	FRESH	GRASS	DESERT	SCRUB	O WOODS	D WOODS	C WOODS	FARMS	TOWNS
Common Flicker	R							X	X	X	X	X	X
Acorn Woodpecker	R								X	X	X		
Lewis' Woodpecker	R					X			X	X	X	X	
White-headed Woodpecker	R										X		
Yellow-bellied Sapsucker	R								X	X	X	X	
Williamson's Sapsucker	R								X		X		
Red-breasted Sapsucker	R								X	X	X		
Hairy Woodpecker	R								X	X	X	X	X
Downy Woodpecker	R								X	X		X	X
Black-backed Woodpecker	R								X		X		

FLYCATCHERS

	SEASON	OCEAN	SHORE	SALT	FRESH	GRASS	DESERT	SCRUB	O WOODS	D WOODS	C WOODS	FARMS	TOWNS
Eastern Kingbird	B					X		X	X			X	X
Western Kingbird	B					X		X	X			X	
Ash-throated Flycatcher	B						X	X	X	X			
Say's Phoebe	B					X		X				X	
Willow Flycatcher	B							X	X	X			
Least Flycatcher	M								X	X			
Hammond's Flycatcher	B										X		
Dusky Flycatcher	B							X	X	X	X		
Gray Flycatcher	B						X	X	X				
Western Flycatcher	B									X	X		
Western Wood Pewee	B								X	X	X	X	
Olive-sided Flycatcher	B								X		X		

LARKS

	SEASON	OCEAN	SHORE	SALT	FRESH	GRASS	DESERT	SCRUB	O WOODS	D WOODS	C WOODS	FARMS	TOWNS
Horned Lark	R		X			X						X	X

SWALLOWS

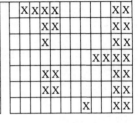

	SEASON	OCEAN	SHORE	SALT	FRESH	GRASS	DESERT	SCRUB	O WOODS	D WOODS	C WOODS	FARMS	TOWNS
Tree Swallow	B		X	X	X	X						X	X
Bank Swallow	B				X	X						X	X
Rough-winged Swallow	B				X							X	X
Violet-green Swallow	B									X	X	X	X
Cliff Swallow	B				X	X						X	X
Barn Swallow	B				X	X						X	X
Purple Martin	B								X			X	X

JAYS & CROWS

	SEASON	OCEAN	SHORE	SALT	FRESH	GRASS	DESERT	SCRUB	O WOODS	D WOODS	C WOODS	FARMS	TOWNS
Steller's Jay	R								X	X	X		
Scrub Jay	R							X	X	X			X
Pinyon Jay	R							X	X	X	X	X	
Gray Jay	R										X		
Black-billed Magpie	R					X		X	X			X	X
Clark's Nutcracker	R										X		
Common Raven	R		X			X	X	X	X	X	X	X	X
Common Crow	R						X		X	X	X		X	X
Northwestern Crow	R		X	X								X	X

TITMICE

	SEASON	OCEAN	SHORE	SALT	FRESH	GRASS	DESERT	SCRUB	O WOODS	D WOODS	C WOODS	FARMS	TOWNS
Black-capped Chickadee	R								X	X	X	X	X	X
Mountain Chickadee	R										X		
Boreal Chickadee	R										X		
Chestnut-backed Chickadee	R										X		
Plain Titmouse	R								X	X		X	X

	SEASON	OCEAN	SHORE	SALT	FRESH	GRASS	DESERT	SCRUB	O WOODS	D WOODS	C WOODS	FARMS	TOWNS
BUSHTITS													
Common Bushtit	R							X	X	X		X	X
DIPPERS													
Dipper	B				X								
NUTHATCHES													
White-breasted Nuthatch	B								X	X	X	X	X
Red-breasted Nuthatch	R								X	X	X		
Pygmy Nuthatch	R										X		
CREEPERS													
Brown Creeper	R									X	X		
WRENS													
House Wren	B							X	X			X	X
Winter Wren	R							X		X	X		
Bewick's Wren	R							X	X			X	
Rock Wren	B						X	X					
Canyon Wren	R							X					
Long-billed Marsh Wren	R			X				X					
THRASHERS													
Mockingbird	B							X	X	X		X	X
Catbird	B								X	X	X	X	X
Sage Thrasher	B						X	X					

	SEASON	OCEAN	SHORE	SALT	FRESH	GRASS	DESERT	SCRUB	O WOODS	D WOODS	C WOODS	FARMS	TOWNS
THRUSHES													
American Robin	R								X	X		X	X
Varied Thrush	R									X	X		
Hermit Thrush	R								X	X	X		
Swainson's Thrush	B								X	X	X		
Gray-cheeked Thrush	M								X	X	X		
Veery	B								X	X			
Western Bluebird	R								X			X	
Mountain Bluebird	R					X			X				
Townsend's Solitaire	R								X		X		
Wrentit	R							X	X				
Golden-crowned Kinglet	R										X		
Ruby-crowned Kinglet	R							X	X	X	X		

	SEASON	OCEAN	SHORE	SALT	FRESH	GRASS	DESERT	SCRUB	O WOODS	D WOODS	C WOODS	FARMS	TOWNS
PIPITS													
Water Pipit	R		X			X						X	X

	SEASON	OCEAN	SHORE	SALT	FRESH	GRASS	DESERT	SCRUB	O WOODS	D WOODS	C WOODS	FARMS	TOWNS
WAXWINGS													
Bohemian Waxwing	R							X	X	X	X	X	X
Cedar Waxwing	R							X	X	X	X	X	X

	SEASON	OCEAN	SHORE	SALT	FRESH	GRASS	DESERT	SCRUB	O WOODS	D WOODS	C WOODS	FARMS	TOWNS
SHRIKES													
Northern Shrike	W				X	X		X				X	
Loggerhead Shrike	R					X	X	X	X			X	

	SEASON	OCEAN	SHORE	SALT	FRESH	GRASS	DESERT	SCRUB	O WOODS	D WOODS	C WOODS	FARMS	TOWNS
STARLINGS													
Starling	R											X	X
Crested Myna	R											X	X

	SEASON	OCEAN	SHORE	SALT	FRESH	GRASS	DESERT	SCRUB	O WOODS	D WOODS	C WOODS	FARMS	TOWNS
VIREOS													
Solitary Vireo	B									X	X		
Hutton's Vireo	R									X	X		
Red-eyed Vireo	B								X	X		X	X
Warbling Vireo	B								X	X		X	X
WARBLERS													
Orange-crowned Warbler	B								X	X	X		
Nashville Warbler	B								X	X	X	X	
Yellow Warbler	B				X				X	X		X	
Yellow-rumped Warbler	R									X	X	X	
Townsend's Warbler	B										X		
Black-throated Gray Warbler	B								X	X	X	X	
Northern Waterthrush	B				X					X	X	X	
Common Yellowthroat	B								X	X		X	
Yellow-breasted Chat	B								X	X			
MacGillivray's Warbler	B								X				
Wilson's Warbler	B								X	X	X		
American Redstart	B								X	X	X		
WEAVER FINCHES													
House Sparrow	R											X	X
BLACKBIRDS													
Bobolink	B				X	X						X	
Western Meadowlark	R					X						X	
Yellow-headed Blackbird	B				X								
Red-winged Blackbird	R			X	X	X						X	
Tricolored Blackbird	B				X	X						X	
Northern Oriole	B									X	X	X	X

BLACKBIRDS, *continued*

	SEASON	OCEAN	SHORE	SALT	FRESH	GRASS	DESERT	SCRUB	O WOODS	D WOODS	C WOODS	FARMS	TOWNS
Brewer's Blackbird	R					X						X	X
Brown-headed Cowbird	B								X			X	X

TANAGERS

	SEASON	OCEAN	SHORE	SALT	FRESH	GRASS	DESERT	SCRUB	O WOODS	D WOODS	C WOODS	FARMS	TOWNS
Western Tanager	B										X		

CARDINALS & BUNTINGS

	SEASON	OCEAN	SHORE	SALT	FRESH	GRASS	DESERT	SCRUB	O WOODS	D WOODS	C WOODS	FARMS	TOWNS
Black-headed Grosbeak	B								X	X		X	
Lazuli Bunting	B							X	X	X		X	

FINCHES

	SEASON	OCEAN	SHORE	SALT	FRESH	GRASS	DESERT	SCRUB	O WOODS	D WOODS	C WOODS	FARMS	TOWNS
Evening Grosbeak	R								X	X	X	X	X
Purple Finch	R									X	X	X	X
Cassin's Finch	R										X		
House Finch	R					X	X	X				X	X
Pine Grosbeak	R										X		
Rosy Finch	R				X								
Hoary Redpoll	W				X							X	
Common Redpoll	W				X	X							
Pine Siskin	R										X	X	
American Goldfinch	R				X		X					X	X
Lesser Goldfinch	R				X		X	X				X	X
Red Crossbill	R										X		
White-winged Crossbill	W										X		

SPARROWS

	SEASON	OCEAN	SHORE	SALT	FRESH	GRASS	DESERT	SCRUB	O WOODS	D WOODS	C WOODS	FARMS	TOWNS
Green-tailed Towhee	B					X	X	X					
Rufous-sided Towhee	R						X	X				X	X

SPARROWS, *continued*

	SEASON	OCEAN	SHORE	SALT	FRESH	GRASS	DESERT	SCRUB	O WOODS	D WOODS	C WOODS	FARMS	TOWNS
Brown Towhee	R							X	X			X	X
Savannah Sparrow	R	X	X			X						X	
Grasshopper Sparrow	B					X						X	
Vesper Sparrow	B					X						X	
Lark Sparrow	B					X		X	X			X	
Sage Sparrow	B						X	X					
Dark-eyed Junco	R								X	X	X	X	X
Tree Sparrow	W					X		X	X			X	
Chipping Sparrow	B					X		X	X			X	X
Brewer's Sparrow	B					X	X	X					
White-crowned Sparrow	R					X		X	X			X	X
Golden-crowned Sparrow	R					X		X	X		X		
Fox Sparrow	R							X		X	X	X	
Lincoln's Sparrow	B					X		X	X	X			
Song Sparrow	R							X			X	X	X
Lapland Longspur	W	X		X	X							X	X
Snow Bunting	W	X				X	X					X	

CHECKLIST OF SOUTHWESTERN BIRDS

	SEASON	OCEAN	SHORE	SALT	FRESH	GRASS	DESERT	SCRUB	O WOODS	D WOODS	C WOODS	FARMS	TOWNS
LOONS													
Common Loon	W	X	X	X	X								
Red-throated Loon	W		X	X	X								
GREBES													
Western Grebe	R			X	X								
Red-necked Grebe	W		X	X	X								
Horned Grebe	W		X	X	X								
Eared Grebe	R		X	X	X								
Pied-billed Grebe	R		X	X	X								
SHEARWATERS													
Pink-footed Shearwater	M	X											
Black-vented Shearwater	M	X	X										
Sooty Shearwater	M	X											
Short-tailed Shearwater	M	X											
Butler's Shearwater	M	X	X										
STORM-PETRELS													
Black Storm-petrel	B	X	X										
Ashy Storm-petrel	B	X	X										
Fork-tailed Storm-petrel	W	X	X	X									
Leach's Storm-petrel	B	X	X										

	SEASON	OCEAN	SHORE	SALT	FRESH	GRASS	DESERT	SCRUB	O WOODS	D WOODS	C WOODS	FARMS	TOWNS
PELICANS													
Brown Pelican	R	X	X	X									
White Pelican	R		X	X	X								
CORMORANTS													
Brandt's Cormorant	R		X	X									
Double-crested Cormorant	R		X	X	X								
Pelagic Cormorant	R	X	X	X									
HERONS & BITTERNS													
Great Blue Heron	R			X	X								
Green-backed Heron	R			X	X								
Cattle Egret	R			X	X	X						X	
Great Egret	R			X	X								
Snowy Egret	R			X	X							X	
Black-crowned Night-heron	R			X	X								
American Bittern	R			X	X								
Least Bittern	R				X								
SWANS													
Tundra Swan	W			X	X	X							
GEESE													
Canada Goose	W			X	X	X						X	
Brant	W		X	X	X	X							
White-fronted Goose	W				X	X							
Snow Goose	W		X	X	X	X							

	SEASON	OCEAN	SHORE	SALT	FRESH	GRASS	DESERT	SCRUB	O WOODS	D WOODS	C WOODS	FARMS	TOWNS
MARSH DUCKS													
Mallard	R			X	X	X							
Pintail	R			X	X								
Gadwall	R			X	X	X							
American Wigeon	W			X	X	X							
Northern Shoveler	W			X	X								
Blue-winged Teal	W			X	X								
Cinnamon Teal	R				X								
Green-winged Teal	R			X	X								
Wood Duck	R				X								
WHISTLING DUCKS													
Fulvous Whistling Duck	R				X	X							X
Black-bellied Whistling Duck	B				X								X
DIVING DUCKS													
Redhead	R			X	X								
Canvasback	W			X	X								
Ring-necked Duck	W			X	X								
Greater Scaup	W		X	X	X								
Lesser Scaup	W		X	X	X								
Common Goldeneye	W		X	X	X								
Barrow's Goldeneye	R		X	X	X								
Bufflehead	W		X	X	X								
Black Scoter	W	X	X	X	X								
White-winged Scoter	W		X	X	X								
Surf Scoter	W	X	X	X	X								
STIFF-TAILED DUCKS													
Ruddy Duck	R			X	X	X							

	SEASON	OCEAN	SHORE	SALT	FRESH	GRASS	DESERT	SCRUB	O WOODS	D WOODS	C WOODS	FARMS	TOWNS
MERGANSERS													
Common Merganser	R			X	X								
Red-breasted Merganser	W	X	X	X									
Hooded Merganser	W			X	X								
VULTURES													
Turkey Vulture	R					X	X		X			X	
Black Vulture	R					X	X		X			X	
California Condor	R					X	X					X	
KITES													
White-tailed Kite	R					X		X					
ACCIPITERS													
Goshawk	R								X	X	X	X	
Cooper's Hawk	R								X	X	X	X	
Sharp-shinned Hawk	R									X	X	X	
HARRIERS													
Northern Harrier	R				X	X						X	
BUTEOS													
Rough-legged Hawk	W					X		X				X	
Ferruginous Hawk	R					X		X					
Red-tailed Hawk	R					X			X	X	X	X	
Red-shouldered Hawk	R					X				X	X	X	
Swainson's Hawk	B				X	X						X	

BUTEOS, *continued*

	SEASON	OCEAN	SHORE	SALT	FRESH	GRASS	DESERT	SCRUB	O WOODS	D WOODS	C WOODS	FARMS	TOWNS
Harris' Hawk	R						X	X	X				
Zone-tailed Hawk	B						X	X	X	X			

EAGLES

	SEASON	OCEAN	SHORE	SALT	FRESH	GRASS	DESERT	SCRUB	O WOODS	D WOODS	C WOODS	FARMS	TOWNS
Golden Eagle	R					X	X	X	X				
Bald Eagle	R	X	X	X	X								

OSPREY

	SEASON	OCEAN	SHORE	SALT	FRESH	GRASS	DESERT	SCRUB	O WOODS	D WOODS	C WOODS	FARMS	TOWNS
Osprey	R		X	X	X								

CARACARA

	SEASON	OCEAN	SHORE	SALT	FRESH	GRASS	DESERT	SCRUB	O WOODS	D WOODS	C WOODS	FARMS	TOWNS
Caracara	R					X	X					X	

FALCONS

	SEASON	OCEAN	SHORE	SALT	FRESH	GRASS	DESERT	SCRUB	O WOODS	D WOODS	C WOODS	FARMS	TOWNS
Prairie Falcon	R					X	X	X					
Peregrine Falcon	R		X			X	X						
Merlin	W		X			X			X		X		
American Kestrel	R					X		X	X			X	
Aplomado Falcon	B					X	X						

GROUSE

	SEASON	OCEAN	SHORE	SALT	FRESH	GRASS	DESERT	SCRUB	O WOODS	D WOODS	C WOODS	FARMS	TOWNS
Blue Grouse	R								X	X	X		
Ruffed Grouse	R								X	X	X	X	
Sage Grouse	R					X	X	X					

	SEASON	OCEAN	SHORE	SALT	FRESH	GRASS	DESERT	SCRUB	O WOODS	D WOODS	C WOODS	FARMS	TOWNS

QUAIL & PHEASANTS

	SEASON	OCEAN	SHORE	SALT	FRESH	GRASS	DESERT	SCRUB	O WOODS	D WOODS	C WOODS	FARMS	TOWNS
Scaled Quail	R								X	X			
California Quail	R					X	X	X				X	X
Gambel's Quail	R						X	X					
Mountain Quail	R							X	X	X	X		
Montezuma Quail	R							X	X	X	X		
Ring-necked Pheasant	R					X		X				X	
Chukar	R					X	X	X					

TURKEYS

	SEASON	OCEAN	SHORE	SALT	FRESH	GRASS	DESERT	SCRUB	O WOODS	D WOODS	C WOODS	FARMS	TOWNS
Wild Turkey	R								X	X	X		

CRANES

	SEASON	OCEAN	SHORE	SALT	FRESH	GRASS	DESERT	SCRUB	O WOODS	D WOODS	C WOODS	FARMS	TOWNS
Sandhill Crane	R				X	X						X	

RAILS

	SEASON	OCEAN	SHORE	SALT	FRESH	GRASS	DESERT	SCRUB	O WOODS	D WOODS	C WOODS	FARMS	TOWNS
Clapper Rail	R			X									
Virginia Rail	R			X	X								
Sora	R			X	X							X	
Yellow Rail	R				X	X						X	
Black Rail	R			X	X								
Common Gallinule (Moorhen)	R				X								
American Coot	R			X	X							X	

	SEASON	OCEAN	SHORE	SALT	FRESH	GRASS	DESERT	SCRUB	O WOODS	D WOODS	C WOODS	FARMS	TOWNS
STILTS & AVOCETS													
American Avocet	R		X	X	X								
Black-necked Stilt	R		X	X	X	X							
PLOVERS													
Semipalmated Plover	W		X	X	X								
Killdeer	R		X	X	X	X						X	
Snowy Plover	R		X	X	X								
Black-bellied Plover	W		X	X	X	X						X	
Mountain Plover	R					X	X						
GODWITS													
Marbled Godwit	W	X	X	X	X								
CURLEWS													
Whimbrel	W	X	X	X	X								
Long-billed Curlew	R	X	X	X	X								
UPLAND SANDPIPERS													
Spotted Sandpiper	R		X	X	X	X							
Willet	W	X	X	X									
Greater Yellowlegs	W				X	X							
Lesser Yellowlegs	W			X	X	X							
SNIPE													
Common Snipe	R				X	X	X						

	SEASON	OCEAN	SHORE	SALT	FRESH	GRASS	DESERT	SCRUB	O WOODS	D WOODS	C WOODS	FARMS	TOWNS

SANDPIPERS

	SEASON	OCEAN	SHORE	SALT	FRESH	GRASS	DESERT	SCRUB	O WOODS	D WOODS	C WOODS	FARMS	TOWNS
Short-billed Dowitcher	W		X	X	X								
Long-billed Dowitcher	W			X	X								
Red Knot	W		X	X	X								
Sanderling	W		X	X	X								
Western Sandpiper	W		X	X	X								
Least Sandpiper	W		X	X	X								
Black Turnstone	W		X	X									
Ruddy Turnstone	W		X	X									
Surfbird	W		X	X									
Dunlin	W		X										

GULLS

	SEASON	OCEAN	SHORE	SALT	FRESH	GRASS	DESERT	SCRUB	O WOODS	D WOODS	C WOODS	FARMS	TOWNS
Glaucous-winged Gull	W	X	X	X									X
Western Gull	R	X	X	X									X
Herring Gull	W		X	X	X	X						X	X
California Gull	R		X	X	X	X							
Ring-billed Gull	W		X	X	X							X	X
Mew Gull	W		X	X	X								
Heermann's Gull	R	X	X	X									
Bonaparte's Gull	W		X	X	X								X
Black-legged Kittiwake	W	X	X										

TERNS

	SEASON	OCEAN	SHORE	SALT	FRESH	GRASS	DESERT	SCRUB	O WOODS	D WOODS	C WOODS	FARMS	TOWNS
Forster's Tern	R			X	X								
Common Tern	M		X	X	X								
Least Tern	B		X	X	X							X	X
Royal Tern	W		X	X									
Elegant Tern	R		X	X									
Caspian Tern	B		X	X	X								
Black Tern	B		X	X	X							X	

	SEASON	OCEAN	SHORE	SALT	FRESH	GRASS	DESERT	SCRUB	O WOODS	D WOODS	C WOODS	FARMS	TOWNS

SKIMMERS
Black Skimmer	B		X	X	X								

ALCIDS
Common Murre	R	X	X										
Pigeon Guillemot	R		X	X									
Tufted Puffin	R	X	X										
Rhinoceros Auklet	R	X	X										
Cassin's Auklet	R	X	X										
Marbled Murrelet	R		X	X							X		

PIGEONS & DOVES
Band-tailed Pigeon	R									X	X		
Rock Dove	R											X	X
White-winged Dove	B					X	X	X				X	X
Mourning Dove	R					X	X	X				X	X
Spotted Dove	R											X	X
Ringed Turtle-dove	R												X
Ground Dove	R					X	X	X			X		
Inca Dove	R					X	X	X				X	X

CUCKOOS
Yellow-billed Cuckoo	B							X	X	X		X	
Roadrunner	R						X	X					

OWLS
Barn Owl	R					X		X	X			X	X

	SEASON	OCEAN	SHORE	SALT	FRESH	GRASS	DESERT	SCRUB	O WOODS	D WOODS	C WOODS	FARMS	TOWNS

OWLS, *continued*

	SEASON	OCEAN	SHORE	SALT	FRESH	GRASS	DESERT	SCRUB	O WOODS	D WOODS	C WOODS	FARMS	TOWNS
Western Screech Owl	R								X	X		X	X
Whiskered Owl	R								X	X			
Flammulated Owl	B										X		
Great Horned Owl	R					X	X	X	X	X	X	X	X
Burrowing Owl	R		X			X	X	X				X	X
Long-eared Owl	R						X	X	X	X	X		
Short-eared Owl	W				X	X		X				X	
Saw-whet Owl	R									X	X		
Pygmy Owl	R									X	X		
Elf Owl	B						X	X	X				

GOATSUCKERS

	SEASON	OCEAN	SHORE	SALT	FRESH	GRASS	DESERT	SCRUB	O WOODS	D WOODS	C WOODS	FARMS	TOWNS
Whip-poor-will	B								X	X		X	
Poor-will	R					X	X	X	X				
Common Nighthawk	B							X				X	X
Lesser Nighthawk	B					X	X	X				X	

SWIFTS

	SEASON	OCEAN	SHORE	SALT	FRESH	GRASS	DESERT	SCRUB	O WOODS	D WOODS	C WOODS	FARMS	TOWNS
Vaux's Swift	B								X	X			
White-throated Swift	R					X	X	X	X	X	X		

HUMMINGBIRDS

	SEASON	OCEAN	SHORE	SALT	FRESH	GRASS	DESERT	SCRUB	O WOODS	D WOODS	C WOODS	FARMS	TOWNS
Broad-tailed Hummingbird	B					X		X	X	X	X		
Rufous Hummingbird	M					X			X	X	X		
Allen's Hummingbird	B					X		X	X				
Calliope Hummingbird	B					X		X	X	X	X		
Anna's Hummingbird	R							X	X			X	X
Costa's Hummingbird	R					X	X	X					

	SEASON	OCEAN	SHORE	SALT	FRESH	GRASS	DESERT	SCRUB	O WOODS	D WOODS	C WOODS	FARMS	TOWNS

HUMMINGBIRDS, *continued*

	SEASON	OCEAN	SHORE	SALT	FRESH	GRASS	DESERT	SCRUB	O WOODS	D WOODS	C WOODS	FARMS	TOWNS
Black-chinned Hummingbird	B						X		X	X			X
Blue-throated Hummingbird	B								X	X	X		
Broad-billed Hummingbird	B						X	X					
Magnificent Hummingbird	B								X	X	X		

KINGFISHERS

	SEASON	OCEAN	SHORE	SALT	FRESH	GRASS	DESERT	SCRUB	O WOODS	D WOODS	C WOODS	FARMS	TOWNS
Belted Kingfisher	R		X	X	X								

WOODPECKERS

	SEASON	OCEAN	SHORE	SALT	FRESH	GRASS	DESERT	SCRUB	O WOODS	D WOODS	C WOODS	FARMS	TOWNS
Common Flicker	R								X	X	X	X	X	X
Gila Woodpecker	R							X	X	X			
Ladder-backed Woodpecker	R							X	X	X	X		X	X
Nuttall's Woodpecker	R							X	X	X			X
Acorn Woodpecker	R								X	X	X		
Lewis' Woodpecker	R						X		X	X	X	X	
White-headed Woodpecker	R									X		
Yellow-bellied Sapsucker	R								X	X	X	X	
Williamson's Sapsucker	R								X		X		
Strickland's Woodpecker	R								X	X		
Hairy Woodpecker	R								X	X	X	X	X
Downy Woodpecker	R								X	X		X	X
Black-backed Woodpecker	R								X		X		
Red-breasted Sapsucker	R								X	X	X		

FLYCATCHERS

	SEASON	OCEAN	SHORE	SALT	FRESH	GRASS	DESERT	SCRUB	O WOODS	D WOODS	C WOODS	FARMS	TOWNS
Eastern Kingbird	B					X		X	X			X	

FLYCATCHERS, *continued*

	SEASON	OCEAN	SHORE	SALT	FRESH	GRASS	DESERT	SCRUB	O WOODS	D WOODS	C WOODS	FARMS	TOWNS
Western Kingbird	B					X		X	X			X	
Cassin's Kingbird	R					X		X	X			X	
Tropical Kingbird	B					X		X	X	X		X	
Vermilion Flycatcher	R							X	X				
Sulphur-bellied Flycatcher	B							X	X	X			
Brown-crested Flycatcher	B						X	X	X	X			
Ash-throated Flycatcher	R						X	X	X	X			
Dusky-capped Flycatcher	B							X	X	X			
Black Phoebe	R				X			X	X			X	X
Say's Phoebe	R					X		X				X	
Willow Flycatcher	B							X	X	X			
Least Flycatcher	M								X	X			
Hammond's Flycatcher	B										X		
Dusky Flycatcher	B							X	X	X	X		
Gray Flycatcher	R						X	X	X				
Western Flycatcher	B									X	X		
Greater Pewee	B										X		
Western Wood Pewee	B								X	X	X	X	
Olive-sided Flycatcher	B								X		X		

LARKS

	SEASON	OCEAN	SHORE	SALT	FRESH	GRASS	DESERT	SCRUB	O WOODS	D WOODS	C WOODS	FARMS	TOWNS
Horned Lark	R		X			X						X	X

SWALLOWS

	SEASON	OCEAN	SHORE	SALT	FRESH	GRASS	DESERT	SCRUB	O WOODS	D WOODS	C WOODS	FARMS	TOWNS
Tree Swallow	R	X	X	X	X							X	X
Bank Swallow	B			X	X							X	X
Rough-winged Swallow	R				X							X	X
Violet-green Swallow	R									X	X	X	X

SWALLOWS, continued

	SEASON	OCEAN	SHORE	SALT	FRESH	GRASS	DESERT	SCRUB	O WOODS	D WOODS	C WOODS	FARMS	TOWNS
Cliff Swallow	B				X	X						X	X
Cave Swallow	B					X	X	X					
Barn Swallow	B				X	X						X	X
Purple Martin	B										X	X	X

JAYS & CROWS

	SEASON	OCEAN	SHORE	SALT	FRESH	GRASS	DESERT	SCRUB	O WOODS	D WOODS	C WOODS	FARMS	TOWNS
Steller's Jay	R								X	X	X		
Scrub Jay	R							X	X	X			X
Gray-breasted Jay	R								X	X			
Pinyon Jay	R							X	X	X	X	X	
Gray Jay	R										X		
Black-billed Magpie	R					X		X	X		X	X	
Yellow-billed Magpie	R					X		X	X	X		X	X
Clark's Nutcracker	R										X		
Common Raven	R	X				X	X	X	X	X	X	X	X
Chihuahuan Raven	R					X	X	X	X			X	
Common Crow	R					X		X	X	X		X	X

TITMICE

	SEASON	OCEAN	SHORE	SALT	FRESH	GRASS	DESERT	SCRUB	O WOODS	D WOODS	C WOODS	FARMS	TOWNS
Black-capped Chickadee	W							X	X	X	X	X	X
Mountain Chickadee	R										X		
Chestnut-backed Chickadee	R										X		
Plain Titmouse	R								X	X		X	X
Bridled Titmouse	R								X	X			

VERDINS

	SEASON	OCEAN	SHORE	SALT	FRESH	GRASS	DESERT	SCRUB	O WOODS	D WOODS	C WOODS	FARMS	TOWNS
Verdin	R						X	X					

	SEASON	OCEAN	SHORE	SALT	FRESH	GRASS	DESERT	SCRUB	O WOODS	D WOODS	C WOODS	FARMS	TOWNS

BUSHTITS

Common Bushtit	R							X	X	X		X	X

DIPPERS

Dipper	B				X								

NUTHATCHES

White-breasted Nuthatch	B								X	X	X	X	X
Red-breasted Nuthatch	R								X	X	X		
Pygmy Nuthatch	R										X		

CREEPERS

Brown Creeper	R									X	X		

WRENS

House Wren	R							X	X			X	X
Winter Wren	R							X		X	X		
Bewick's Wren	R							X	X			X	
Cactus Wren	R						X	X					
Rock Wren	R						X	X					
Canyon Wren	R							X					
Long-billed Marsh Wren	R				X			X					

THRASHERS

Mockingbird	R							X	X	X		X	X
Bendire's Thrasher	R							X	X				

THRASHERS, *continued*

	SEASON	OCEAN	SHORE	SALT	FRESH	GRASS	DESERT	SCRUB	O WOODS	D WOODS	C WOODS	FARMS	TOWNS
Curve-billed Thrasher	R						X	X					
California Thrasher	R							X	X			X	X
LeConte's Thrasher	R						X	X					
Crissal Thrasher	R						X	X					
Sage Thrasher	R						X	X					

THRUSHES

	SEASON	OCEAN	SHORE	SALT	FRESH	GRASS	DESERT	SCRUB	O WOODS	D WOODS	C WOODS	FARMS	TOWNS
American Robin	R							X	X			X	X
Varied Thrush	W									X	X		
Hermit Thrush	R								X	X	X		
Swainson's Thrush	B								X	X	X		
Veery	B								X	X			
Western Bluebird	R								X		X		
Mountain Bluebird	R					X			X				
Townsend's Solitaire	R								X		X		
Wrentit	R							X	X				
Blue-gray Gnatcatcher	R							X	X	X			
Black-tailed Gnatcatcher	R						X	X					
Golden-crowned Kinglet	R										X		
Ruby-crowned Kinglet	R							X	X	X	X		

PIPITS

	SEASON	OCEAN	SHORE	SALT	FRESH	GRASS	DESERT	SCRUB	O WOODS	D WOODS	C WOODS	FARMS	TOWNS
Water Pipit	R		X		X							X	X
Sprague's Pipit	W				X							X	

WAXWINGS

	SEASON	OCEAN	SHORE	SALT	FRESH	GRASS	DESERT	SCRUB	O WOODS	D WOODS	C WOODS	FARMS	TOWNS
Cedar Waxwing	W							X	X	X	X	X	X

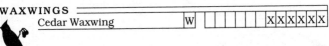

	SEASON	OCEAN	SHORE	SALT	FRESH	GRASS	DESERT	SCRUB	O WOODS	D WOODS	C WOODS	FARMS	TOWNS

SILKY-FLYCATCHERS

	SEASON	OCEAN	SHORE	SALT	FRESH	GRASS	DESERT	SCRUB	O WOODS	D WOODS	C WOODS	FARMS	TOWNS
Phainopepla	R						X	X					

SHRIKES

	SEASON	OCEAN	SHORE	SALT	FRESH	GRASS	DESERT	SCRUB	O WOODS	D WOODS	C WOODS	FARMS	TOWNS
Loggerhead Shrike	R					X	X	X	X			X	

STARLINGS

	SEASON	OCEAN	SHORE	SALT	FRESH	GRASS	DESERT	SCRUB	O WOODS	D WOODS	C WOODS	FARMS	TOWNS
Starling	R											X	X

VIREOS

	SEASON	OCEAN	SHORE	SALT	FRESH	GRASS	DESERT	SCRUB	O WOODS	D WOODS	C WOODS	FARMS	TOWNS
Gray Vireo	B					X	X	X					
Solitary Vireo	B								X	X			
Bell's Vireo	B							X					
Hutton's Vireo	R								X	X			
Warbling Vireo	B								X	X		X	X

WARBLERS

	SEASON	OCEAN	SHORE	SALT	FRESH	GRASS	DESERT	SCRUB	O WOODS	D WOODS	C WOODS	FARMS	TOWNS
Orange-crowned Warbler	R							X	X	X			
Nashville Warbler	B							X	X	X	X		
Virginia's Warbler	B							X	X	X	X		
Lucy's Warbler	B						X	X					
Yellow Warbler	B				X			X	X			X	
Yellow-rumped Warbler	R							X	X	X	X		
Townsend's Warbler	W										X		
Black-throated Gray Warbler	R							X	X	X	X		
Grace's Warbler	B										X		
Common Yellowthroat	R							X	X			X	

WARBLERS, *continued*

	SEASON	OCEAN	SHORE	SALT	FRESH	GRASS	DESERT	SCRUB	O WOODS	D WOODS	C WOODS	FARMS	TOWNS
Yellow-breasted Chat	B							X	X				
MacGillivray's Warbler	B							X					
Wilson's Warbler	R							X		X			
Red-faced Warbler	B										X		
American Redstart	W							X	X	X			
Painted Redstart	R									X	X		

WEAVER FINCHES

	SEASON	OCEAN	SHORE	SALT	FRESH	GRASS	DESERT	SCRUB	O WOODS	D WOODS	C WOODS	FARMS	TOWNS
House Sparrow	R											X	X

BLACKBIRDS

	SEASON	OCEAN	SHORE	SALT	FRESH	GRASS	DESERT	SCRUB	O WOODS	D WOODS	C WOODS	FARMS	TOWNS
Eastern Meadowlark	R					X						X	
Western Meadowlark	R					X						X	
Yellow-headed Blackbird	R			X									
Red-winged Blackbird	R			X	X	X						X	
Tricolored Blackbird	R				X	X						X	
Scott's Oriole	B						X	X	X				
Hooded Oriole	B							X				X	X
Northern Oriole	B								X	X		X	X
Brewer's Blackbird	R					X						X	X
Great-tailed Grackle	R			X			X					X	X
Brown-headed Cowbird	R									X		X	X
Bronzed Cowbird	R					X		X				X	

TANAGERS

	SEASON	OCEAN	SHORE	SALT	FRESH	GRASS	DESERT	SCRUB	O WOODS	D WOODS	C WOODS	FARMS	TOWNS
Western Tanager	B								X	X			
Summer Tanager	B							X	X	X			
Hepatic Tanager	B								X	X			

CARDINALS & BUNTINGS

	SEASON	OCEAN	SHORE	SALT	FRESH	GRASS	DESERT	SCRUB	O WOODS	D WOODS	C WOODS	FARMS	TOWNS
Cardinal	R							X	X			X	X
Pyrrhuloxia	R						X	X					
Black-headed Grosbeak	B								X	X		X	
Blue Grosbeak	B							X				X	
Indigo Bunting	B							X	X			X	
Lazuli Bunting	R							X	X	X		X	
Painted Bunting	B							X	X				

FINCHES

	SEASON	OCEAN	SHORE	SALT	FRESH	GRASS	DESERT	SCRUB	O WOODS	D WOODS	C WOODS	FARMS	TOWNS
Evening Grosbeak	R								X	X	X	X	X
Purple Finch	R									X	X	X	X
Cassin's Finch	R										X		
House Finch	R					X	X	X				X	X
Pine Grosbeak	R										X		
Rosy Finch	R				X								
Pine Siskin	R									X	X		
American Goldfinch	R					X		X				X	X
Lesser Goldfinch	R					X		X	X			X	X
Lawrence's Goldfinch	R					X			X				
Red Crossbill	R										X		

SPARROWS

	SEASON	OCEAN	SHORE	SALT	FRESH	GRASS	DESERT	SCRUB	O WOODS	D WOODS	C WOODS	FARMS	TOWNS
Green-tailed Towhee	R							X	X	X			
Rufous-sided Towhee	R							X	X			X	X
Brown Towhee	R							X	X			X	X
Abert's Towhee	R							X	X	X		X	X
Savannah Sparrow	R		X	X		X						X	
Grasshopper Sparrow	R					X						X	
Lark Bunting	W					X						X	

SPARROWS, *continued*

	SEASON	OCEAN	SHORE	SALT	FRESH	GRASS	DESERT	SCRUB	O WOODS	D WOODS	C WOODS	FARMS	TOWNS
Vesper Sparrow	R					X						X	
Lark Sparrow	R					X		X	X			X	
Black-throated Sparrow	R						X						
Sage Sparrow	R						X	X					
Dark-eyed Junco	R								X	X	X	X	X
Yellow-eyed Junco	R										X		
Rufous-crowned Sparrow	R					X		X	X				
Cassin's Sparrow	R					X	X	X					
Tree Sparrow	W					X		X	X			X	
Chipping Sparrow	R					X		X	X			X	X
Clay-colored Sparrow	W					X		X					
Brewer's Sparrow	R					X	X	X					
White-crowned Sparrow	R					X		X	X			X	X
Golden-crowned Sparrow	W					X		X	X		X		
White-throated Sparrow	W							X	X	X	X	X	X
Fox Sparrow	R							X		X	X	X	
Lincoln's Sparrow	R					X		X	X	X		X	
Song Sparrow	R		X	X	X			X	X	X		X	X
McCown's Longspur	W				X							X	
Chestnut-collared Longspur	W				X							X	
Lapland Longspur	W		X		X	X						X	X

CHECKLIST OF ALASKAN BIRDS

	SEASON	OCEAN	SHORE	SALT	FRESH	GRASS	DESERT	SCRUB	O WOODS	D WOODS	C WOODS	FARMS	TOWNS
LOONS													
Common Loon	R	X	X	X									
Red-throated Loon	R		X	X	X								
GREBES													
Red-necked Grebe	R		X	X	X								
Horned Grebe	R		X	X	X								
SHEARWATERS													
Pink-footed Shearwater	M	X											
Sooty Shearwater	M	X											
Short-tailed Shearwater	M	X											
STORM-PETRELS													
Fork-tailed Storm-petrel	R	X	X	X									
Leach's Storm-petrel	R	X	X										
CORMORANTS													
Double-crested Cormorant	R		X	X	X								
Pelagic Cormorant	R	X	X	X									
HERONS													
American Bittern	B			X	X								

	SEASON	OCEAN	SHORE	SALT	FRESH	GRASS	DESERT	SCRUB	O WOODS
SWANS									
Tundra Swan	B			X	X	X			
Trumpeter Swan	R			X	X	X			
Whooper Swan	M			X	X	X			
GEESE									
Canada Goose	B			X	X	X			
Brant	B	X	X						
Emperor Goose	R	X	X			X			
White-fronted Goose	B				X	X			
MARSH DUCKS									
Mallard	B			X	X	X			
Pintail	B			X	X				
Gadwall	B			X	X	X			
American Wigeon	B			X	X	X			
Northern Shoveler	B			X	X				
Green-winged Teal	B			X	X				
Falcated Teal	M		X	X	X				
DIVING DUCKS									
Redhead	B			X	X				
Canvasback	B			X	X				
Ring-necked Duck	B			X	X				
Greater Scaup	R		X	X	X				
Lesser Scaup	B		X	X	X				

DIVING DUCKS, continued

	SEASON	OCEAN	SHORE	SALT	FRESH	GRASS	DESERT	SCRUB	O WOODS	D WOODS	C WOODS	FARMS	TOWNS
Tufted Duck	M		X	X	X								
Common Goldeneye	R		X	X	X								
Barrow's Goldeneye	R		X	X	X								
Bufflehead	R		X	X	X								
Harlequin Duck	R		X	X	X								
Common Eider	R		X	X									
King Eider	R		X	X	X								
Steller's Eider	R		X	X									
Oldsquaw	R	X	X	X	X	X							
Black Scoter	R	X	X	X	X								
White-winged Scoter	R		X	X	X								
Surf Scoter	R	X	X	X	X								

MERGANSERS

	SEASON	OCEAN	SHORE	SALT	FRESH	GRASS	DESERT	SCRUB	O WOODS	D WOODS	C WOODS	FARMS	TOWNS
Common Merganser	R			X	X								
Red-breasted Merganser	R		X	X	X								
Hooded Merganser	B			X	X								

ACCIPITERS

	SEASON	OCEAN	SHORE	SALT	FRESH	GRASS	DESERT	SCRUB	O WOODS	D WOODS	C WOODS	FARMS	TOWNS
Goshawk	R								X	X	X	X	
Sharp-shinned Hawk	B								X	X	X		

HARRIERS

	SEASON	OCEAN	SHORE	SALT	FRESH	GRASS	DESERT	SCRUB	O WOODS	D WOODS	C WOODS	FARMS	TOWNS
Northern Harrier	B				X	X							X

BUTEOS

	SEASON	OCEAN	SHORE	SALT	FRESH	GRASS	DESERT	SCRUB	O WOODS	D WOODS	C WOODS	FARMS	TOWNS
Rough-legged Hawk	B					X		X					X

BUTEOS, continued

	SEASON	OCEAN	SHORE	SALT	FRESH	GRASS	DESERT	SCRUB	O WOODS	D WOODS	C WOODS	FARMS	TOWNS
Red-tailed Hawk	B					X		X	X	X		X	
Swainson's Hawk	B				X	X						X	

EAGLES

	SEASON	OCEAN	SHORE	SALT	FRESH	GRASS	DESERT	SCRUB	O WOODS	D WOODS	C WOODS	FARMS	TOWNS
Golden Eagle	B					X	X	X	X				
Bald Eagle	R	X	X	X									

OSPREY

	SEASON	OCEAN	SHORE	SALT	FRESH	GRASS	DESERT	SCRUB	O WOODS	D WOODS	C WOODS	FARMS	TOWNS
Osprey	B		X	X	X								

FALCONS

	SEASON	OCEAN	SHORE	SALT	FRESH	GRASS	DESERT	SCRUB	O WOODS	D WOODS	C WOODS	FARMS	TOWNS
Gyrfalcon	R		X			X							
Peregrine Falcon	B		X			X	X						
Merlin	B		X			X			X		X		
American Kestrel	B					X		X	X			X	

GROUSE

	SEASON	OCEAN	SHORE	SALT	FRESH	GRASS	DESERT	SCRUB	O WOODS	D WOODS	C WOODS	FARMS	TOWNS
Blue Grouse	R								X	X	X		
Spruce Grouse	R										X		
Ruffed Grouse	R								X	X	X	X	
Sharp-tailed Grouse	R					X			X	X			
Willow Ptarmigan	R					X		X					
Rock Ptarmigan	R					X							
White-tailed Ptarmigan	R					X							

	SEASON	OCEAN	SHORE	SALT	FRESH	GRASS	DESERT	SCRUB	O WOODS	D WOODS	C WOODS	FARMS	TOWNS
CRANES													
Sandhill Crane	B				X	X						X	
OYSTERCATCHERS													
Black Oystercatcher	R	X	X										
PLOVERS													
Semipalmated Plover	B		X	X	X								
Killdeer	B		X			X	X					X	
Lesser Golden Plover	B		X	X	X	X						X	
Black-bellied Plover	B		X	X	X	X						X	
GODWITS													
Bar-tailed Godwit	B		X	X	X								
Hudsonian Godwit	B		X	X	X								
CURLEWS													
Whimbrel	B		X	X	X	X							
Bristle-thighed Curlew	B		X	X		X							
UPLAND SANDPIPERS													
Upland Sandpiper	B					X						X	
Buff-breasted Sandpiper	B					X						X	

	SEASON	OCEAN	SHORE	SALT	FRESH	GRASS	DESERT	SCRUB	O WOODS	D WOODS	C WOODS	FARMS	TOWNS

UPLAND SANDPIPERS, *continued*

	SEASON	OCEAN	SHORE	SALT	FRESH	GRASS	DESERT	SCRUB	O WOODS	D WOODS	C WOODS	FARMS	TOWNS
Wood Sandpiper	B		X	X		X							
Solitary Sandpiper	B				X								
Spotted Sandpiper	B		X	X	X	X							
Wandering Tattler	B		X	X	X								
Greater Yellowlegs	B				X	X							
Lesser Yellowlegs	B			X	X	X							

PHALAROPES

	SEASON	OCEAN	SHORE	SALT	FRESH	GRASS	DESERT	SCRUB	O WOODS	D WOODS	C WOODS	FARMS	TOWNS
Red Phalarope	B	X	X			X							
Red-necked Phalarope	B	X	X		X	X							

SNIPE

	SEASON	OCEAN	SHORE	SALT	FRESH	GRASS	DESERT	SCRUB	O WOODS	D WOODS	C WOODS	FARMS	TOWNS
Common Snipe	B				X	X	X						

SANDPIPERS

	SEASON	OCEAN	SHORE	SALT	FRESH	GRASS	DESERT	SCRUB	O WOODS	D WOODS	C WOODS	FARMS	TOWNS
Short-billed Dowitcher	B		X	X	X								
Long-billed Dowitcher	B			X	X								
Red Knot	B		X	X	X	X							
Semipalmated Sandpiper	B		X	X	X	X							
Western Sandpiper	B		X	X	X	X							
Least Sandpiper	B		X	X	X	X							
Black Turnstone	B		X	X									
Ruddy Turnstone	B		X	X		X							
Surfbird	B		X	X									
Rock Sandpiper	R		X			X							
Dunlin	B		X			X							

JAEGERS & SKUAS

	SEASON	OCEAN	SHORE	SALT	FRESH	GRASS	DESERT	SCRUB	O WOODS	D WOODS	C WOODS	FARMS	TOWNS
Parasitic Jaeger	B	X	X			X							

GULLS

	SEASON	OCEAN	SHORE	SALT	FRESH	GRASS	DESERT	SCRUB	O WOODS	D WOODS	C WOODS	FARMS	TOWNS
Glaucous Gull	R		X	X	X								X
Glaucous-winged Gull	B	X	X	X									X
Herring Gull	B		X	X	X	X						X	X
Mew Gull	R		X	X	X								
Bonaparte's Gull	B		X	X	X								X
Black-legged Kittiwake	B	X	X										
Red-legged Kittiwake	R	X	X										
Sabine's Gull	B	X	X			X							

TERNS

	SEASON	OCEAN	SHORE	SALT	FRESH	GRASS	DESERT	SCRUB	O WOODS	D WOODS	C WOODS	FARMS	TOWNS
Arctic Tern	B	X	X			X							
Aleutian Tern	R	X	X	X									

ALCIDS

	SEASON	OCEAN	SHORE	SALT	FRESH	GRASS	DESERT	SCRUB	O WOODS	D WOODS	C WOODS	FARMS	TOWNS
Common Murre	W	X	X										
Thick-billed Murre	R		X										
Pigeon Guillemot	R		X	X									
Horned Puffin	R	X	X										
Tufted Puffin	R	X	X										
Rhinoceros Auklet	R	X	X										
Crested Auklet	R	X	X										
Least Auklet	R	X	X										
Cassin's Auklet	B	X	X										

ALCIDS, *continued*

	SEASON	OCEAN	SHORE	SALT	FRESH	GRASS	DESERT	SCRUB	O WOODS	D WOODS	C WOODS	FARMS	TOWNS
Marbled Murrelet	R		X	X							X		
Kittlitz's Murrelet	R	X	X										
Parakeet Auklet	R	X	X										

OWLS

	SEASON	OCEAN	SHORE	SALT	FRESH	GRASS	DESERT	SCRUB	O WOODS	D WOODS	C WOODS	FARMS	TOWNS
Great Horned Owl	R					X	X	X	X	X	X	X	X
Snowy Owl	R		X	X	X	X							
Hawk-owl	R										X		
Great Gray Owl	R					X				X	X		
Short-eared Owl	B				X	X		X			X		
Boreal Owl	R										X		

GOATSUCKERS

	SEASON	OCEAN	SHORE	SALT	FRESH	GRASS	DESERT	SCRUB	O WOODS	D WOODS	C WOODS	FARMS	TOWNS
Common Nighthawk	B				X			X				X	X

HUMMINGBIRDS

	SEASON	OCEAN	SHORE	SALT	FRESH	GRASS	DESERT	SCRUB	O WOODS	D WOODS	C WOODS	FARMS	TOWNS
Rufous Hummingbird	B				X				X	X	X		

KINGFISHERS

	SEASON	OCEAN	SHORE	SALT	FRESH	GRASS	DESERT	SCRUB	O WOODS	D WOODS	C WOODS	FARMS	TOWNS
Belted Kingfisher	R		X	X	X								

WOODPECKERS

	SEASON	OCEAN	SHORE	SALT	FRESH	GRASS	DESERT	SCRUB	O WOODS	D WOODS	C WOODS	FARMS	TOWNS
Common Flicker	R							X	X	X	X	X	X
Red-breasted Sapsucker	R								X	X	X		
Hairy Woodpecker	R								X	X	X	X	X

WOODPECKERS, *continued*

	SEASON	OCEAN	SHORE	SALT	FRESH	GRASS	DESERT	SCRUB	O WOODS	D WOODS	C WOODS	FARMS	TOWNS
Downy Woodpecker	R								X	X		X	X
Black-backed Woodpecker	R								X		X		

FLYCATCHERS

	SEASON	OCEAN	SHORE	SALT	FRESH	GRASS	DESERT	SCRUB	O WOODS	D WOODS	C WOODS	FARMS	TOWNS
Say's Phoebe	B					X		X				X	
Alder Flycatcher	B							X	X	X			
Hammond's Flycatcher	B								X	X			
Western Flycatcher	B								X	X			
Western Wood Pewee	B							X	X	X	X		
Olive-sided Flycatcher	B								X		X		

LARKS

	SEASON	OCEAN	SHORE	SALT	FRESH	GRASS	DESERT	SCRUB	O WOODS	D WOODS	C WOODS	FARMS	TOWNS
Horned Lark	B		X			X						X	X

SWALLOWS

	SEASON	OCEAN	SHORE	SALT	FRESH	GRASS	DESERT	SCRUB	O WOODS	D WOODS	C WOODS	FARMS	TOWNS
Tree Swallow	B		X	X	X	X						X	X
Bank Swallow	B				X	X						X	X
Violet-green Swallow	B								X	X	X	X	
Cliff Swallow	B				X	X						X	X
Barn Swallow	B				X	X						X	X

JAYS & CROWS

	SEASON	OCEAN	SHORE	SALT	FRESH	GRASS	DESERT	SCRUB	O WOODS	D WOODS	C WOODS	FARMS	TOWNS
Steller's Jay	R								X	X	X		
Gray Jay	R										X		
Black-billed Magpie	R					X		X	X			X	X
Common Raven	R	X			X	X	X	X	X	X	X	X	
Northwestern Crow	R	X	X									X	X

	SEASON	OCEAN	SHORE	SALT	FRESH	GRASS	DESERT	SCRUB	O WOODS	D WOODS	C WOODS	FARMS	TOWNS
TITMICE													
Black-capped Chickadee	R								X	X	X	X	X	X
Boreal Chickadee	R										X		
Chestnut-backed Chickadee	R										X		
Siberian Chickadee	R							X	X	X	X		
DIPPERS													
Dipper	B				X								
NUTHATCHES													
Red-breasted Nuthatch	R									X	X	X		
CREEPERS													
Brown Creeper	R										X	X		
WRENS													
Winter Wren	R								X		X	X		
THRUSHES													
American Robin	B								X	X			X	X
Varied Thrush	R										X	X		
Hermit Thrush	B									X	X	X		
Swainson's Thrush	B									X	X	X		
Gray-cheeked Thrush	B									X	X	X		

	SEASON	OCEAN	SHORE	SALT	FRESH	GRASS	DESERT	SCRUB	O WOODS	D WOODS	C WOODS	FARMS	TOWNS

THRUSHES, *continued*

	SEASON	OCEAN	SHORE	SALT	FRESH	GRASS	DESERT	SCRUB	O WOODS	D WOODS	C WOODS	FARMS	TOWNS
Mountain Bluebird	B					X			X				
Townsend's Solitaire	B								X		X		
Bluethroat	B					X	X						
Wheatear	B					X							
Golden-crowned Kinglet	B										X		
Ruby-crowned Kinglet	B							X	X	X	X		
Arctic Warbler	B								X	X	X		

PIPITS & WAGTAILS

	SEASON	OCEAN	SHORE	SALT	FRESH	GRASS	DESERT	SCRUB	O WOODS	D WOODS	C WOODS	FARMS	TOWNS
Water Pipit	B		X		X							X	X
Yellow Wagtail	B		X		X	X		X				X	

WAXWINGS

	SEASON	OCEAN	SHORE	SALT	FRESH	GRASS	DESERT	SCRUB	O WOODS	D WOODS	C WOODS	FARMS	TOWNS
Bohemian Waxwing	B							X	X	X	X	X	
Cedar Waxwing	B							X	X	X	X	X	X

SHRIKES

	SEASON	OCEAN	SHORE	SALT	FRESH	GRASS	DESERT	SCRUB	O WOODS	D WOODS	C WOODS	FARMS	TOWNS
Northern Shrike	R				X	X			X			X	

STARLINGS

	SEASON	OCEAN	SHORE	SALT	FRESH	GRASS	DESERT	SCRUB	O WOODS	D WOODS	C WOODS	FARMS	TOWNS
Starling	R											X	X

WARBLERS

	SEASON	OCEAN	SHORE	SALT	FRESH	GRASS	DESERT	SCRUB	O WOODS	D WOODS	C WOODS	FARMS	TOWNS
Orange-crowned Warbler	B							X	X	X			
Yellow Warbler	B				X			X	X			X	
Yellow-rumped Warbler	B							X	X	X	X		

	SEASON	OCEAN	SHORE	SALT	FRESH	GRASS	DESERT	SCRUB	O WOODS	D WOODS	C WOODS	FARMS	TOWNS

WARBLERS, *continued*

	SEASON	OCEAN	SHORE	SALT	FRESH	GRASS	DESERT	SCRUB	O WOODS	D WOODS	C WOODS	FARMS	TOWNS
Townsend's Warbler	B										X		
Blackpoll Warbler	B								X	X	X		
Northern Waterthrush	B				X				X	X	X		
Common Yellowthroat	B							X	X	X		X	
MacGillivray's Warbler	B									X			
Wilson's Warbler	B							X	X	X			

BLACKBIRDS

	SEASON	OCEAN	SHORE	SALT	FRESH	GRASS	DESERT	SCRUB	O WOODS	D WOODS	C WOODS	FARMS	TOWNS
Red-winged Blackbird	B		X	X	X								X
Rusty Blackbird	B			X					X	X	X		

TANAGERS

	SEASON	OCEAN	SHORE	SALT	FRESH	GRASS	DESERT	SCRUB	O WOODS	D WOODS	C WOODS	FARMS	TOWNS
Western Tanager	B									X	X		

FINCHES

	SEASON	OCEAN	SHORE	SALT	FRESH	GRASS	DESERT	SCRUB	O WOODS	D WOODS	C WOODS	FARMS	TOWNS
Pine Grosbeak	R										X		
Gray-crowned Rosy Finch	R					X							
Hoary Redpoll	R					X						X	
Common Redpoll	R					X	X						
Pine Siskin	R									X	X		
Red Crossbill	R										X		
White-winged Crossbill	R										X		

SPARROWS

	SEASON	OCEAN	SHORE	SALT	FRESH	GRASS	DESERT	SCRUB	O WOODS	D WOODS	C WOODS	FARMS	TOWNS
Savannah Sparrow	B		X	X		X						X	
Dark-eyed Junco	B								X	X	X	X	X
Tree Sparrow	B				X			X	X			X	

SPARROWS, *continued*

	SEASON	OCEAN	SHORE	SALT	FRESH	GRASS	DESERT	SCRUB	O WOODS	D WOODS	C WOODS	FARMS	TOWNS
Chipping Sparrow	B					X		X	X			X	X
White-crowned Sparrow	B					X		X	X			X	X
Golden-crowned Sparrow	B					X		X	X		X		
Fox Sparrow	B							X		X	X	X	
Lincoln's Sparrow	B					X		X	X	X		X	
Song Sparrow	R		X	X	X			X	X	X		X	X
Lapland Longspur	B		X		X	X						X	X
Snow Bunting	R		X			X						X	
McKay's Bunting	W		X			X							

PART IV

NOTEBOOK

DATE: _____   TIME: _____

LOCATION: _____

HABITAT: _____

WEATHER: _____

BIRDS: _____

_____

_____

_____

_____

BEHAVIOR: _____

_____

DATE: _____ TIME: _____

LOCATION: _____

HABITAT: _____

WEATHER: _____

BIRDS: _____

_____

_____

_____

_____

BEHAVIOR: _____

_____

DATE: _____   TIME: _____

LOCATION: _____

HABITAT: _____

WEATHER: _____

BIRDS: _____

_____

_____

_____

_____

BEHAVIOR: _____

_____

DATE: _____ TIME: _____
LOCATION: _____
HABITAT: _____
WEATHER: _____
BIRDS: _____
_____
_____
_____
_____
BEHAVIOR: _____
_____

DATE: _____ TIME: _____

LOCATION: _____

HABITAT: _____

WEATHER: _____

BIRDS: _____

_____

_____

_____

_____

BEHAVIOR: _____

_____

DATE: _____   TIME: _____

LOCATION: _____

HABITAT: _____

WEATHER: _____

BIRDS: _____

_____

_____

_____

_____

BEHAVIOR: _____

_____

DATE: _____   TIME: _____

LOCATION: _____

HABITAT: _____

WEATHER: _____

BIRDS: _____

_____

_____

_____

_____

BEHAVIOR: _____

_____

DATE: _____ TIME: _____

LOCATION: _____

HABITAT: _____

WEATHER: _____

BIRDS: _____

_____

_____

_____

_____

BEHAVIOR: _____

_____

DATE: _____ TIME: _____

LOCATION: _____

HABITAT: _____

WEATHER: _____

BIRDS: _____

_____

_____

_____

_____

BEHAVIOR: _____

_____

DATE: _____   TIME: _____

LOCATION: _____

HABITAT: _____

WEATHER: _____

BIRDS: _____

_____

_____

_____

_____

BEHAVIOR: _____

_____

DATE: _____   TIME: _____

LOCATION: _____

HABITAT: _____

WEATHER: _____

BIRDS: _____

_____

_____

_____

_____

BEHAVIOR: _____

_____

DATE: _____   TIME: _____

LOCATION: _____

HABITAT: _____

WEATHER: _____

BIRDS: _____

_____

_____

_____

_____

BEHAVIOR: _____

_____

DATE: _____   TIME: _____

LOCATION: _____

HABITAT: _____

WEATHER: _____

BIRDS: _____

_____

_____

_____

_____

BEHAVIOR: _____

_____

DATE: _____   TIME: _____

LOCATION: _____

HABITAT: _____

WEATHER: _____

BIRDS: _____

_____

_____

_____

_____

BEHAVIOR: _____

_____